BOXED IN

BY

JOHNNIE E. SANDERS

PREFACE

If you feel as if you're in a fight, coming out of a fight or headed toward a fight, I wrote this book for you, because I think we thrive in adversity; when the situation is at its absolute worse, in a period of do or die, when we feel boxed in as if there's no choice. That's when we are actually willing and open to re-thinking the way we do things and what we accept.

In the most extreme condition, we have to continue to fight to remind ourselves that this day is not our last day, we're not done, it's not over UNTIL WE ARE DEAD.

Throughout life, limits are tested to learn the technique to get beyond them. Overcoming the bad circumstance, the odds and the obstacles, is a sensation greater than anything easily gained. Adversity can be beaten into an opportunity – into a victory.

CHAPTER 1
CUDA BAY

There I was, in the umpteen bank, for the umpteen time, trying to attain a loan, to keep my business afloat during the worse recession the country had experienced since the great depression. On the contrary, my textile, shoes and apparel manufacturing company actually was one, doing above average until my company hit a financial wall. My company was too young to have the well-established cash flow needed. My retail customers were taking longer and longer to pay. "Everyone is holding on to cash as long as they can."

"Your credit line is maxed out. How can I help you?" The loan officer seemed sympathetic, but he hadn't said yes or no to my loan.

"Sir, I'm willing to take unconventional steps. How about a loan based on money owed by my customers to me; my accounts receivable? ... My company regularly collects hundreds of thousands of dollars from big, well-known stores. My retail customers may not be real fast paying, but they do pay."

"Mr. Bay, we just don't have the infrastructure or manpower to monitor each borrower's customers to make sure not only your invoices, but also their invoices, are up to snuff. We are a typical community bank and do not have a department set aside to do that."

I masked my anger, listening, while eyeing the procedural operations of the bank; checking my watch once seeing the cash cow going from teller to teller, timing it from beginning until it was back inside the vault.

"Sir, my company has had six consecutive years of profits. I employ close to 350 people from this community. I and this community need this loan." I'd conveyed my sincerest request, but his reaction was skeptical.

"Mr. Bay, this type of loan wouldn't be appropriate to grant. I have to deny your loan."

I was pissed, but I understood the system in which we lived; Why would he come to an ethical judgement? There wasn't a positive incentive for him to behave ethically. Our laws set a minimum standard for behavior. Ethics set a higher standard of behavior.

.....

I lived in a community where the minority was the majority, in the city of Philadelphia. The neighborhood's blocks encompassed the gutter to the filthy rich. I had been at the bottom but was now fortunate to live on the upper end of the hood. It was all due to the strength of my wife. She'd stayed by my side while I had served an eleven-year federal sentence and had used what resources I'd left to bring our dreams alive; a business and a home: Self-reliance. She had it waiting for me when I returned.

I was released eight years ago. All Courtney wanted was a child and my complete devotion. I'd rededicated my vows to her, and we'd produced CB2, our five-year-old son.

Courtney and I were determined not to allow our company's financial crunch to affect us away from the factory, but it had. First, we had to start back working 12 to 14 hour shifts, which ate into our time spent with CB2. We were fortunate to have my mother in law to relieve some of the stress. Still more stress flowed over and made its way to our late-night discussions.

"They wouldn't give me the time of day."

"In a few months we won't be able to make payroll." Courtney was the accountant, so there

wasn't a way to hide anything concerning the financial status of the company from her.

I'd met my wife when she was fresh out of college, still excited about tomorrow and what the world had to offer.

"I talked to some old friends, that'll float me the cash for pennies on the dollar."

She was still beautiful, but life had taken her innocence and replaced it with suspicion, that showed in her eyes. I wasn't willing to discuss any further details, so I rolled over with my back to her.

.....

I'd been labelled the angry black man by many that found it comfortable to suffer peacefully, because I had opened a study hall based on the science of religion; a forum to re-educate through multi avenues of communication: Visually thinking, re-thinking religious teachings, social mores, habits – all the things that contribute to social control of conduct.

During my eleven years of incarceration I'd received a BS in psychology and a minor in civilization, and a minor in theology. I had continued my education with a masters' degree in mythology and a doctorate degree in history. I was qualified to be angry and to lecture, which had narrowed down to Friday and Saturday evenings, since I was working so many hours in the factory.

I'd made certain the outside appearance of the study hall had no resemblance to a synagogue, mosque or church, nothing to do with a house of worship or prayer. I'd copied and used the architectural design of the most modern library's entrance.

Inside there were virtually several glass rooms with the latest technology, which made a corridor leading to an amphitheater, where I lectured, "... We don't go to heaven! We bring heaven down to earth. Our father which presides in heaven as on earth. ..." From the ceiling hung a screen for creative visualization, which was important because what we associate in our minds we bring to life.

My ushers, just as distinguished and well-groomed as I was, in their designer suits, took their positions at all entrances as the lights were dimmed.

"... The authority of your will, your mind, positive or negative is the controlling factor. You can't get mad without the use of your imagination. You amp yourself up by breathing hard, then you picture what you're going to do next ..."

.....

Four heavily armed masked men, dressed in designer suits, shoes and gloves, stormed the community bank. Two immediately jumped over the counter and stopped the manager from pushing the cash cow into the vault. The rounds let off from the M4 automatic assault rifle made everyone comply. Everything on the cash cow was quickly dumped into two bags. The masked figures then dashed to an awaiting minivan. The two bags of cash were dumped into two buckets of water, then covered as the minivan sped off. The dye packs exploded, but rose to the top of the water. A metal detector wane was waved over the stacks of cash taken out of the water. It sounded over the tracking devices, which were thrown out of the window.

.....

"... I raise the simple question; is this normal? Is this acceptable, and are there any plans to reduce the imbalance? When a people, an institution or a country can live with a disease so long that we have come to accept it as normal – you know we are in trouble. ... My heart is fixed. I must be about my people's work. My words, my actions, my deeds should be proof. Due to the misuse of our imagination is our short coming. The imagination is a door way to pull those actions to manifest into reality. ..."

Five ushers replaced the others that were guarding the entrances. I made eye contact with one to the right of me, then continued my lecture. "... The word appropriate is thrown around a lot. This word is as vague as often. Is it appropriate to teach African American children false history, such as; Columbus discovered America, Lincoln freed the slaves, Egypt is in the middle east, and African American history began on a plantation in 1620? Why was it appropriate for Pope Julius II to authorize Michael Angelo to paint Jesus from Black to white? What time period was it? It was

1505. What was happening in 1505? The slave trade was taking place. How can you enslave African people with Jesus being Black? The Pope, the church, the government, all knew the spirit of the people wouldn't accept slavery with a Black Christ. So the enemy became the deity. That what was sacred to us they destroyed, made ugly. Once it was destroyed, they taught us to laugh at anything linked to Africanism. So we would only want the western culture. ..."

CHAPTER 2
PRINCE

Prizefighter, a metaphor to life; a fair fight for what you want. An opportunity versus the devastation of being the misfortunate. Such an allure to poor young boys and men from the ghettos of the world that draw them to boxing gyms, looking for a better life and willing to try to earn it with their fists.

Nubs' gym, nothing modern. No digital machines, just iron, steel and leather. You could see where the dumbbells had been wielded and the bags patched. The air always reeked of body odor. Sweat, blood and dreams stained the weight benches and the mats of the rings. Nubs' gym looked as grimy and dreary and as brutal as the sport of boxing itself. A throwback to boxing days of old. A gateway out of the slums. I'd looked in and entered the gateway when I was a tall chubby eight-year-old. My dad had just gotten a life sentence for beating a man to death, that turned out to be an off duty dirty cop. I couldn't articulate my emotions back then, things were either hard or soft, and I thought I was soft because I was crying to myself a lot. Nothing seemed fair. Hitting the bags and lifting weights were comforting and healing while being in the ring was a relief where I could fight back, be as salvage and brutal as I saw the world.

Years of Nubs' coaching had honed my skills. He'd seen I was full of fight and silently hungry. Nubs was an old prizefighter, that had seen the prize, but wasn't allowed to have it. He only had an index finger and a thumb on his right hand. Some say it was because in the 70's Nubs threw a fight or didn't throw a fight, but the bookies got even either way. Nubs had used what prize money he'd saved to open his gym, and had come close with many contenders to reaching the grand prize. I'd become his protege, his student. Over an eight-year period Nubs had patiently in a dogmatic way trained me by vigorously repeating a series of fundamental drills in a precise manner.

Time had hardened Nubs' outlook and changed his approach to his prize; the world championship title. He understood boxing was more business than a sport. But meanwhile, boxing had become a sweet science to me, but Nubs kept me at amateur status, feeding me, "You ain't there. You need more bouts to get that excellence. You're almost there."

Nubs was a salt and peppered goatee having, bald headed, say whatever he felt, sounding like a pimp one second and a deacon the next; he knew I knew I was ready. I'd grown into a 6'7", 251 pound, 17-year-old with less than four percent body fat, that could knockout my opponent with my left or right jab.

"Kid, you know you're great. It's more to it than boxing. We've got to make the world love you. We can do this by winning the gold in the Olympics. Then you're have a straight shot to the belts."

I respected his boxing sense, and had allowed his dream to mingle in to mine.

"Now focus." Nubs was always a step ahead of me, holding the ropes to the ring as I entered to spar. "Focus! Focus!"

I shot a wicked combination; a liver then a head shot, followed by another liver shot, that folded my sparring partner who dropped to both of his knees.

Nubs jumped the ropes like an energetic child, ecstatic and proud, grabbing me, stopping me from throwing another punch. "Kid! Kid! That's enough! That's enough! Hit the showers."

.....

Nubs had hired me to do the little things around the gym; mopping, emptying the trash, scrubbing and spraying down the showers; a deal he and I had agreed upon to put a few dollars in my pocket per week, so I could focus more on boxing and school instead of a real part time job. The shower room was big enough for an eight-man rotation, and to clean it was a workout in itself.

Nubs' closed at eight every night. I would be done with my cleaning by nine o'clock. The gym was only seven blocks from my home, but Brooke, my girlfriend would be there waiting in her car outside the gym. Philly really didn't have a gang problem, but each block was its own click, and blocks were beefing. So Brooke had made it her duty to be there. She was a tribal beauty, a six foot, 149 pound, blue berry black with almond shaped eyes and sparkling white teeth. She was so fine and pretty, grown men didn't care that she was only 17 and still in high school. Many would've killed or given their last cent to have her, but she and I had made a pact in the sixth grade, promising it would only be us.

The closer we got to a scheduled fight, the more anxious Nubs became. He and I would lock up the gym together for safety concerns. My relationship with Nubs was more than a coach and an athlete, but not quite a father and son thing. Nubs was more of a crazy uncle figure, that was cool, but didn't cut any corners with you – and kept everything raw and in its simplest form.

"You have a big fight Friday. No sex. That means head too." He spoke loud enough to make sure Brooke overheard.

Brooke's car was an older model, a late 90's something, and it was too small for both of us. She'd worked and paid for it herself, as a clerk in an Asian owned clothing store until the owner's wife realized the owner was mesmerized by Brooke.

I was 17, the idea of sex draining my energy was absurd. I knew all of Brooke's soft spots, and she couldn't fend me off while she was driving.

"Stop! You heard Nubs. Stop Prince! You make me sick!" Her words were harsh, but the sinister smirk she gave me let me knew her appetite was the same as mine.

"You know how I get before a fight. C'mon."

We had a secret secluded parking spot, where no one could see inside the car or would bother us, while we used the car as a hotel room.

.....

It was Summer time, so the blocks were alive all day and night. The block I lived on, the homes were neatly kept, narrow, elongated three stories houses, with not much of a front yard and less than a yard apart. I entered my home to be attacked by my youngest sister, Phoenix, a nine-year-old fire ball. She was a new born when our father had gone to prison, so instead of being a daddy's girl, our bond was that same love or stronger.

"You're late! We have to do your ab workout, so a gut check won't drop you." She threw a combination of punches to my stomach, that I faked like had knocked the air out of me. She was my heart. She enjoyed me tossing her around, then over my shoulder as I went toward the kitchen.

"Boy, will stop treating her like she's a boy! Put her down!"

The voice of my mother demanded respect, and the sternness of her eyes let you know there would be consequences if she didn't get it.

"C'mon mama! He ain't …"

"What did you say?"

Phoenix corrected her sentence. "He's not going to drop me. Prince is strong enough to lift us all."

I kissed my mother's cheek and goose-berried her. "Stop! Prince! Stop! I don't know where your lips have been. Smelling like Brooke. Your food is ready."

My mother was angelic, beyond beautiful. Her olive brown complexion and greenish brown eyes had people assuming she was cut; black and some other kind of race. People made the same assumption about every member of my family. We all were splitting images of our parents; our mother and father both looked Creole. My dad was a giant of a man. I remembered placing my hand in my father's hand, asking would mine one day be as big.

"Pharaoh come do these dishes! Phihiem come take out this trash! I'm not telling you again!" Our mother was the general of our family.

At 12 and 14, both of my baby brothers were taller than my mother who wasn't short. She was six feet.

"Phelisa, I'm so glad you were open. I didn't have a thing to wear to the concert. Child you're a lifesaver. Thank you too Precious for hooking us up!" Some people I didn't know, came down from the third floor of our home, which was a department store for men, women and children. The best of the best for the low low.

My family's financial survival depended on the income from my mother's unauthorized store, which was supplied by teams of boosters who sold my mother the merchandise for 20 percent of the price tag or whatever my mother talked them down to.

Precious, my 16-year-old sister, almost identical to my mother, except our mother outweighed her by thirty pounds. Precious helped ran the store. She was the salesperson, coordinating the gear for the customers. Precious had an eye for fashion, along with a millionaire's attitude and openly flossy ways. She sat at the table staring at me, while our mother escorted the customers to the door.

Precious was semi jealous of the closeness between Phoenix and myself. She and I had been very close until our father had died. The prison said our father had hung himself, but the autopsy showed he'd been beaten to death, then hung. We both took the death differently. She'd become calculating, and boxing was my relief valve.

"What do you need me to do this time?"

"Just get the fight over with as fast as possible. I don't trust the owner of the club where we're promoting your-after-party."

"Who do you trust?"

She looked a little hurt, then smiled. "You."

.....

My mother was family centric and made sure we all supported each other. My brothers and Phoenix were too young to sit ringside, so they were made assistant trainers, but stayed in the dressing room. From my notoriety gained from boxing and the respect shown to me in the streets, my brothers worshipped me. In the dressing room they would imitate my intensity, silently bobbing to mental music while Phoenix studied Nubs who took my ear buds out of my ears, shouting his instructions for the one-thousand-time.

"Remember your overhand right combo. He's a sitting duck for it." Phoenix mimicked Nubs' gut to head combo.

I loved rap music. I put my ear buds back in and zoned out while Nubs finished taping my hands. Then a kiss from Phoenix and two hard pounds from my brothers. It was a ritual we performed each fight before I headed toward the ring.

I had tunnel vision; I could only see the ring, the ref, my opponent and his corner team, everyone else and everything else were blacked out, only the sound of rap blasted in my head.

The bell would sound, and I would mentally teleport the fight to another dimension; afloat in space, only two warriors and the occasional arm and voice of the ref and the thunderous voice of Nubs from nowhere and everywhere, "Now! Now!"

CHAPTER 3
CUDA BAY

The building that was now my factory had been an old decrepit warehouse. It was huge, and once renovated, perfectly suited our means. The entrance opened into an elegant showroom, displaying the merchandise. A sale representative was always on hand, managing the computer and phone.

The main area was open; four sections with six subsections, two hundred and sixty-five sewing machines, combining pieces to make a whole. We kept down overhead by paying piece rate versus hourly wages, whichever was the greatest.

There were eight quality control inspectors in each section along with a mechanic and a foreman.

Upstairs were the business and payroll offices and the fashion room, where our designers and engineer hatched their creativity. Courtney had stolen the assistant designers from several of the best designers in the fashion industry.

The heart that pumped the life force throughout the company was our sales reps. Courtney again had lured the next to the best, of the best, with the highest commission rates, plus the quality of our merchandise was top-notch and easy to sell. We'd built a strategy room just to meet with the sale reps twice a month. Business had gone so well, so fast, that we were having growing pains. All of our sales reps were seasoned vets and well connected. They didn't have to pitch, only suggestions and the orders flowed in.

Even though it was early Summer, our designers and engineers were putting on a winter line semi fashion show and lecture, describing the fabrics, the cuts, the reasoning behind every detail of the clothes and the stylish and sturdy structure and comfort of the shoes.

Once I saw that my sales reps were happy with what they'd seen, I stood, "I would like to thank you all for such a good job and if there's no other item needing to be discussed, I'll see you ..."

"Excuse me. There's one thing I'll like to discuss. It's feedback from my regulars. They say they're only receiving 75 percent of their reorders. Can you check into that?"

I was the factory manager. I knew what went out and came in.

"Has anyone else had this feedback?" The majority of the sales team nodded,

"Apologize, but assure them that at the time of their reorders, we filled it to the best of the inventory on hand would allow, for the timing within the season. Thanks for the great job. Keep up the good work."

The retailers were taking advantage of the consignment deal Courtney had used to attain easier placement in their stores. The retailers had a complete quarter of a year to pay for the merchandise and could reorder as many times as possible as long as the items were in stock. The bigger chain, retailers were stocking every store, then waited to the last second or up to a month after the quarter to pay, which had caused my company's cash flow shortage.

.....

My office had a view of the parking lot in the back of the building, and it overlooked the common area of the factory. I opened my office door to see my wife sitting at my desk, on my PC. On the screen I could see she was going over the books.

"What's wrong with your computer in your office?"

"I came over to discuss these angel investors."

"That's exactly what they are."

"Okay. Who are they?"

"It doesn't matter to me who they are."

"Fine! The health insurance cost ate it all, anyway." She typed in hedge fund and asset-based lenders for the cash deposits.

"The quarter ends tomorrow. Use the consignment payments."

"That's needed to cover the material that's been ordered. We need to down size or cut medical coverage all together."

The medical coverage was one of the bright spots of the company, helping those who on their own wouldn't be able to afford medical coverage, which would've been 100 percent of the employees.

"We've discussed this already."

.....

Problem, cause, solution, implementation. This time instead of going directly to the banks, I went to a SBA, a small business association with the hopes they could direct me to a grant or a loan. I received the same double talk from the clerk. "The type of loan you're requesting is different. This type of thing is usually done in a backroom in private."

"No. This would be a legal transaction. Just enter the information and see if any bank is willing to buy the accounts."

"Mr. Bay, this isn't a broker's house. We can't help you."

The term different and deficient are not synonymous. Insecure people believe that if something is different, it's deficient in some way. I left the building mad but determined to think of a means to come up with the cash. I'd lectured; your intellect and imagination equal your personality and your physical actions, which are you; so I tunneled my energy to think of a new innovative way to get the resources needed.

For days I paid for expensive lunches with high profiled athletes and actors and actresses; people with a disposable income but known capitalists. I was blown off, made to wait, then cancelled or told by the ones that did show up, "I'm not in the business of spending money. I'm in the business to make money."

"If you invest in this company eventually you'll make a hundred times more than you would from an endorsement."

"Mr. Bay thanks for the meal, but I'm not interested in investing in your company."

I sat there angry, but I understood people have a frightening capacity to follow what is to be considered the normal order and to shy away from new innovative concepts.

.....

The five hours of the study hall being opened was for just that; studying. The format was similar to school, but a mediator and an instructor were assigned to the classes because of the critical thinking approach. I had banned the military approach of break people down then building them back up; the system of teaching most institutions believe is the best way to teach.

The study subjects were science, astrology, herbaceous, civilization, psychology, mythology and engineering, communication, arts and philosophy. The ages of the members ranged from seven to eighty-one. There were over two hundred members, mostly my employees and their spouse and family members or friends. Unexpectedly the younger generation had embraced the philosophy of the study hall; they could see the problem was with the failing system, not the black man and woman.

I would sit in on the discussions of each group; the study hall was encouraging and supportive to not only the youth but the adults as well.

.....

My lectures consisted of digital slides, visual references to corroborate the facts in my lecture. The ushers would dim the lights, then take their position at the entrances.

"... They say; Black folks sold Black folks into slavery, so we can't blame the white man for slavery. Who is this they? Is the they; people who ancestors owned slaves and got rich off of the labor of slaves or the trade of slave? ... We must follow the chronology of history that rewards all research. Let us go back to Prince Henry the navigator, he sent his men down the West coast of Africa. The first thing they did was kidnap Africans from off the coast of Moratanga. They then sold these Africans to Pope Martin the V; in other words; they sold slaves to the church. So the whole intention of the Europeans were the kidnapping of Africans and enslaving us. Then when DeAugo Asseboa came down the West coast of Africa with approximate 600 men, believe it or not another European was with him named Christopher Columbus. They told the King Ansa, we're coming here to build a castle, asking could they. The king wanted to know why in my land. They said for trading. King Ansa said no. Then DeAugo Asseboa said if you don't allow us to build this castle, we have big guns, that can destroy you and your village that are called cannons. And we will, take you and your people to be traded.

Okay, the plot thickens. DeAugo Asseboa said to the king, but we can give you some guns, so you can go to other villages and bring us people to be traded instead of you. It's documented the Europeans' stolen technology; killing devices had enough force to motivate the survivors to go into the villages of the Aumuga and the Dejarra and kidnap them. So, they gave them guns and rum and told them if they didn't bring these Africans to them, then they would be the ones enslaved. Guns and Rum. This created a havoc, chaos where slavery did not exist. Then came other European nations; The Dutch, the Portuguese, they gave other villages guns and rum to kidnap you. What they did was gave rum and guns to enslave us. It was between Spain, the Dutch and the Portuguese, using Africans to fight each other and whoever won, slaves were gained. And because of our ignorance of making the victim the perpetrator; we say Africans sold Africans into slavery. Can't we see, that it worked so well, that the inner cities that they want back now. ..."

.....

The heavily armed designer suits robbers were in the process of a bank robbery. Everyone in the bank was complying. A security guard was couched in a corner with his gun drawn, trying to build up the nerves to be a hero. The robbers had bagged the money off of the cash cow and were headed toward the entrance when the security guard stepped out with his gun aimed at their chest. His adrenaline rush had him screaming, scared and jittery. "Put your hands up! Don't ..."

The guard's nervousness made him shoot at the sight of the robbers raising their hands with the gun in them.

The bullet proof armor under the designer suit absorbed the shot, but the bullets from the M4 riddled open the security guard's chest.

.....

An usher, exchanging disks in the projector, made eye contact with me, then

gave a nod before returning to his post. "...
So, they've created gangs. And they're
giving one group of brothers guns and
drugs and other groups guns and drugs to
create chaos and havoc. The same thing
that was done on the west coast of Africa.
Now it's the west coast, east coast, gulf
coast and the Midwest of America that
they're experimenting with, and all we can
say is Black on Black crime or violence.
Did the indigenous native of this country
kill off themselves? No. The blood thirsty
Europeans did that single handedly but
buried the facts with lies called American
history. But in order to destroy a people
you make them look like the perpetrator of
themselves. They then taught us to hate
ourselves even more through the divide and
conquer. That's where victims become the
perpetrators. ..."

CHAPTER 4

PRECIOUS

I'm Precious. Prince is my older brother. We're close but had been closer. After the death of our father, I'd become more protective and possessive. Prince had become introverted except when he was in the boxing ring. He had a showmanship as if he'd transformed from his quiet humble self into the ultimate warrior who possessed the cunning, the agility, the power and the patience to devour an opponent at any time during the bout.

I was with my mother and my boyfriend, Shey, cheering and screaming, supporting Prince at his boxing match. Despite the violence surrounding the sport, and everything else too; the viciousness, the blood, the steep rows of seats ascending from the ring, the stench of liquor, weed and cigar smoke that filled the air, the horrible show of fashion by the so-called ballas and the women strutting in high heels, none of it bothered me or my mother. What we saw was 5000 people had turned out for an amateur fight to see my brother who was known for administering brilliant but brutal beatings. His performance was crowd pleasing; flash and flair, blood and guts, regardless how crude and barbaric it was, you couldn't look away. Prince's style captivated the audience. Boxing was my brother's ticket to the land of riches and he would be able to pull our family from the poverty, violence, drugs, crime and other dangers of the industrial wasteland of Philly.

The fight was a very impressive third round knockout for Prince, but instead of the sport reporters focusing on my brother, giving him his due respect, they gathered around Mr. Frank Bosco, a high profiled fight promoter and manager, along with his son, the Hammer, the heavy weight top contender of the world; the great white hope.

"Hammer, are you ready for the Bruiser? ... Hammer, you're scouting the up and coming Prince? ..."

Shey and my mother were in the ring hugging and congratulating Prince. I was furious that my brother was being overlooked, so much that I began banging on the bell until even the people leaving stopped and gave me their attention.

"That's more like it! All heil to his majesty, Prince! Sure he made it look too easy, but it's because he's so great!"

The reporters blew me off and went back at the Hammer.

I banged the bell again.

"Ask him; who ran him out of the amateur ranks, made him give up his dreams of going to the Olympics."

.....

It was an upscale struggling but elegant restaurant during the day, so it was cheap to rent as a night club from ten to two at night; making it the perfect place for Prince's victory celebration slash going off to college party for Shey. A small venue compared to the normal places we'd used to promote parties, but its atmosphere absolutely fitted what I was going after; a setting for family and friends, except I underestimated the number of Prince's fans who thought fans and friends were synonymous. And I didn't know Shey had as many friends.

The place was packed. Bottles popping, loud music and lots of hugs. Shey had filled so many voids in my life. I loved him and he cherished me. He looked square, but to anyone who paid close attention to details, it was obvious how fine polished he was. Nothing Gotti, but the best of everything. An eighteen-year-old man, laid back with the calm intellect of 50 years of experience; That was Shey demeanor. When people saw him, they really didn't, because that's how he wanted; inconspicuous, it was the key to his success. Many who saw us together wondered why, how could we be, our styles were so contrasting. Unknown to most, Shey was the man, his way of thinking before reacting, his respect and courtesy. At first glance I was struck by his rich dark skin and deep jet black wavy hair and his flawless million-dollar smile, plus the fact he could afford to do the things I was dreaming of.

It had taken almost two years for Shey to come clean with me that he dealt heroin, and his promotion company was a way to clean his money. If he hadn't told me, I don't think I would've believed it or ever found out. Prince had hinted at it to me in a warning, but he wasn't certain because of the success of Shey's parties and concerts. Shey had taught me the promotion game, allowing me to handle the clubs, but he handled the concerts. He was my safety valve, but he'd helped me to find my independence, shown me the connections to establish my name as a promoter, given me confidence.

My eyes were sharp. I could distinguish the real from the fake; people and clothes and jewelry. There were a lot of imitations and knock offs, wannabes hungry for an opportunity to be, people trying to get next to Shey. I wanted all of Shey's attention, but it was his time to shine, so I accepted playing the background and watched the door while Shey mingled and played the gracious host.

A crew entered. New Yorkers, somewhat refusing to be waned by the bouncers. Shey quickly made his way to the door, intervening, not letting anything get out of hand. "These are my VIP's. I've got them."

Four huge Columbians; I could tell they were the muscle by the way they guarded a man thin enough and pretty enough to be a woman but fly and distinguished. He resembled an older Marc Anthony. He and Shey greeted each other with a hug and smiles; closeness and respect.

"I didn't think you would make it."

I'd seen the man the night of Shey's graduation, but Shey hadn't introduced me. He'd distant me from them as he did again and led the man off to a secluded area. I could tell by Shey's body language they were discussing something serious.

"Find a replacement or just do it during the breaks or better yet, come home on the weekends and handle things."

"I'm cool man. I'm done."

Both their eyes locked, reading the other. "Nothing I do or say will change your mind?" A simple shake of the head. "You know I love you like a son. I only wish the best for you."

Another hug, then the thin man's crew led the way toward the exit. I knew the guy had to be important. He'd made a trip from New York for a five-minute meeting. I got a good look at him as they passed. Shey stopped me from staring by taking my hand and leading me to the dance floor. I had learned not to ask questions because it pushed Shey away, but by being silent he would eventually confide in me.

The look in Shey's eyes was of joy, a peacefulness, and his touch was so tenderly arousing.

"I love you Precious."

"I love you too." I was about to kiss him when I spotted Brooke, popping bottles and showing all of her teeth, being extra friendly with one of Shey's balla-friends, while a group of boxing fans had Prince's attention across the room. "Let me handle something. I'll be right back."

I left Shey on the dance floor, then grasped Brooke's arm, manhandling her as I pulled her away from the guys. "Bitch, I will beat your muthafuckin' ass if I ever again catch you disrespecting my brother. Now go over there and stick to him like glue." I shoved her in the direction of Prince.

My brother wasn't soft. He was just one of those people that didn't complain. He would deal with things until he could solve it. It was strange, physicalness was a last result for him, the opposite for me.

.....

The warmth of flesh on flesh. The salty sweet taste of sweat. The delightful excruciating pleasure of sex. It was as if it was our first time together and we wanted to make sure it wouldn't be the last. Shey and I both were exhausted, lying in each other's arms at Shey's house. I was scared again, thinking I would be alone again when Shey went off to college. He and my mother were my only friends. No one else understood me or I couldn't stand being around anyone else for an extended period of time.

I'd met Shey at a Young Black Entrepreneurs of America Meeting when I was 13. My mother had made me go to get me out of her hair. Shey had asked what type of business I was thinking of starting. I'd tried to ignore him, but he wouldn't allow me. What caught my interest was when he'd said; think of money like air, it's enough in the world for us to live, share and to enjoy it together. It links us together. Let us make it together."

Shey had taught me everything he knew except the dope game. I was lying there thinking of a way to ask him to allow me to take over his heroin business. I just said it. "Babe, let me take over your business?"

"You've already taken over the business." Narrowing his eyes, studying me in the semi dark room.

"Not that business."

"What other business are you speaking of Precious?"

It wasn't a teachable moment, but I pressed on. "You know."

"No, I don't. I don't know what you're talking about, unless you tell me."

"Teach me the heroin business."

He changed completely. Before I knew it, he'd snatched me out of the bed. "Have you lost your mind! Why in the hell would you ask some shit like that!"

Before I could try to pull away he'd shoved me across the bed so hard that I hit the floor. We were both naked. I didn't have time to recover from the fall before he'd grabbed and pushed me against the wall. The impact knocked the breath out of me. Tears had started falling from my eyes. This was the love of my life. Shey had never raised his voice at me let alone his hand. He threw me on the couch in the lounge part of the bedroom. I loved him, but I wasn't a punk and wasn't about to let him to beat me. He saw me running for my purse and snatched me in the opposite direction, bouncing me off another wall.

Since I couldn't get to my gun, I tried to get his guns. I knew his hiding spots around the room. He was big on being prepared and always thinking. I was his reflection and he knew it. He was quicker, bigger and stronger, blocking my way to each spot, pushing me around, "You want to kill me! You would kill me? ..."

I couldn't win, but I couldn't give up. I couldn't give up. My mother had slept with me for six months after we found out my father had died, convincing me my father hadn't given up but was killed; because Battles don't give up, we fight until we die. I grabbed the lamp which was too heavy for me to fully swing, but it made Shey back up.

"... The dope game isn't safe for men! So every muthafucka with a dick in the game will try you! And if you're not ready to kill to defend what's yours and yourself, you'll end up dead! ..." The light reflected, and I realized he was crying, "... I love you Precious. We have enough money to put both of us through college and buy a house down south, plus start any business you want."

I dropped the lamp and he embraced me. "... I'm not going to college to find anyone new."

"What if you do? Then what?"

"You're all I want. We're going to get married as soon as you graduate high school."

CHAPTER 5

PRINCE

Because of my father's known reputation as an enforcer and collector, and the circumstances of his death and my mother's known supplemental business, when we did attend church, it was demoralizing; the staring and gossiping, by the same people who came to my mother on credit or to borrow money. So my family had basically given up on all forms of religions plus struggling to be above the poverty line had a way of making you believe in only reality.

My mother hated the saying; it is, what it is or must be meant to be. "Hell naw! Show me where it's written in stone! It is what you make it! Get your behind to that study hall."

At first my mother used to have to make me attend the study hall sessions. I didn't think I needed it, boxing had lifted my self-discipline and self-esteem and my confidence, but I didn't have a choice. I was only ten. The kids there looked rough but were smart and eager to answer the questions. My age group was from eight to twelve and was taught in a collective manner by a man, that was patient and concerned; Cuda Bay. He made my experience pleasant. The study hall was a place where I felt accepted and secure.

Due to nurturing, I'd been a member for almost eight years, studying, listening and continuing to learn as most of the members of my group.

"What are our seven principles?"

My class always answered collectively. "Umoja; unity! Kujichaqulia, self-determination! Ujima; collective work and responsibility! Ujamaa; cooperative economics! Kuumba; creativity! Nia; purpose! Imani; faith!"

"What are the seven cardinal virtues of Maat?"

"Truth, justice, order, harmony, balance, reciprocity and righteousness!"

Cuda Bay's ideology of manhood was based on the pyramid. The three angles represented spiritual, mental and physical development.

"Men! Men who have a solid understanding of their history do not make asinine statements such as I'm Black. I'm not an African. Men understand; their culture is Black, and their nationality is of African descent. Men value themselves and their culture."

.....

The power of peer pressure, in a positive or negative form, whichever way manipulated; is the number one influence of youth. Since inner circle of my study group had all read about the tribal rites of passage, plus the lectures from Cuda Bay on rites of passage; focusing on developing boys to men; academically, economically and politically, by being involved in the community socially – over the years we had created our own rites of passage. It was six of us from our class. We'd all become close knit friends. We were fearless soldiers with no orders, boys wanting to be men, wanting to be involved with the solution. We'd become jackers. We knew the streets and we fed on rapists, drug dealers and thieves, home invaders; anyone that was killing the community.

We'd clicked up after the study session. "Pee. O was right about Shey."

"I'm telling you, Shey isn't dealing drugs. He's a promoter. Once upon a time, maybe. But not anymore. He's going off to school to major in pre-med."

"If he still is, is he free game?"

"Shey isn't a damn mark! He's like my family!"

"Dude gave Shey up as his connect last night."

The information had me off balance. I wasn't lying. Shey was like family. My sister loved him. My family loved him for sparking something inside Precious that made her glow, plus his virtues were admirable. I couldn't choose community over my family.

"We can't be making decisions on an impulse. Dude could've been lying to save his ass."

"Or telling the truth to save his ass."

"MO, we're not going to make any hasty decisions. We're going to exercise more caution and scout him out. But, the rules apply if he's dealing. Right? MO?"

MO was our word for my oneness. I couldn't answer. I walked off, thinking boxing was the only reason I wasn't more active in the capers as I rethought the few I had been involved in.

CHAPTER 6

PRECIOUS

It was one day before Shey was scheduled to leave, going to start the Summer mini-semester at Morehouse. He'd promised to spend Sunday with me and my mother; a full day. He'd arrived at the house about 11:30 and had sat in the den with my brothers and Phoenix until one o'clock. Shey looked a little up tight when my mother and I entered the room. Prince's expression was weird too. I could tell something was wrong between them.

"What's up?"

"Why don't you and moms, wait here and I'll be back within an hour?"

"That's a nopie. The only waiting we're doing is in the car while you make your stop. You promised us."

My mother called to Phoenix, "Are you coming? We're going shopping for dresses."

"I don't want any more dresses. I want another pair of Jordan's."

"I'm not buying you another pair of sneakers!"

My mother and I were working on getting Phoenix to be more feminine. She was so tomboyish.

"I'm staying to help Prince do his sit ups and pushups."

"If we're going, we need to go. So we'll miss the church traffic."

My mother made eye contact with Prince, her way of seeing if it was fine for Phoenix to hangout with him.

Prince was eyeing Shey while answering our mother. "They're going to the gym with me."

"I love you all. Have fun at the gym and don't get in Nubs' way. Prince, take care of my babies." She always gave goodbye kisses, just in case it was the last time.

Shey was in the Phantom. He only pulled it out when he had something special planned. It was too flashy for his taste, but I'd coached him into buying it.

My mother loved the car. "We're not arguing over who is riding in the front seat. Just, just get in the back seat Precious."

She pulled rank, but I liked seeing my mother shine, because she was always putting us, her children before her.

"After I make my quick stop. I need you ladies to be kind of quick with the shopping. I have a surprise scheduled."

We got caught in the church traffic. Church had just let out, then there was an accident that made the traffic come to a complete halt; a guy on a bike had been hit by a car, three cars ahead of us.

There were cars behind us to the end of the block. My mother was impressed by how luxurious the inside of the car was, changing the temperature of the AC on her side of the car. Shey had become impatient but the cars were bumper to bumper, too close for us to back up to turn around. Shey saw them; masked figures coming. The 9mm from under his seat was already in his hand but Shey also spotted the masked figures approaching from the passenger side. Instead of putting up a fight and endangering my mother and my life, Shey tossed his gun out of the window, then pressed a button that opened the trunk.

"It's in the trunk man. You can have it. There's no need for anyone to get hurt."

Shey pressed another button on the radio and revealed a stash spot, where the gym bag that contained the heroin was located. One masked figure opened the bag. "Yo Mo. No ends, just that shit!"

"Where's the money?"

"That's money to me."

I noticed the masked figure over Shey, making eye contact with the one holding the gun on my mother, then gave a head nod. Before Shey could grab another gun from the door pouch, the explosion, then the blood from my mother's head splashed on him. Shey was raising the gun. I could only scream as I saw the fire coming from the 9mm aimed at Shey's face. I opened the door on the one with a gun on me, but the figure kicked the door close, then shot. I remember the fire then the darkness.

CHAPTER 7

PRINCE

It was a little after nine o'clock when my brothers, Phoenix and I returned home from the gym. It was strange to find no one there. The house was exactly like we had left it. No dinner had been prepared, and my beans and rice that were in the slow cooker, were almost out of water. My mother had and OCD that made her consistent with everything she did. The whole situation was unusual. I put together a quick but huge meal, then made my brothers and Phoenix take their baths. I was a little concerned about my mother and Precious' whereabouts, but my rationale was since it was Shey's last day in town, he'd done something special with them.

The later it got the more my concerns became worries. I woke up my brothers off of the den's floor. "Go get into your beds."

I carried Phoenix to her bedroom.

I then tried calling my mother and Precious' cell phones, both calls went straight to their voice mail. I couldn't sleep, so I stayed in the den doing sit ups. The movie ended, and the late-night local news came on. Tibbets of clips of the main stories were being flashed to catch your attention before a commercial came on. The image of yellow tap around a new Phantom stayed in my head. It was the last event reported on before going to the weather.

"Reports of a carjacking turned fatal due to a traffic jam. The driver was pronounced dead on the scene, two other passengers are in critical condition from gunshot wounds."

I hadn't seen Shey's car, but the one on the news was Precious' style. I frantically called the television station. "... Which hospital were the people in the carjacking, taken to? ... Because they're my family members! ... Saint Mary's. Thank you."

I immediately called Brook but got her voice mail. I texted her with 911.

My phone rang, and it was her, pretending to be asleep until hearing, "I need you to take us to the hospital."

"Give me twenty minutes and I'll be there." It hadn't occurred to me that she wasn't at home.

.....

Saint Mary's was a private catholic hospital, one of the best in the state. Normally the ambulance would've taken anyone from Philly to Central Mercy, the county hospital, but since the shooting had happened on the out skirts of the city, my mother and sister had the good fortune to be taken to a finer hospital.

The emergency room was quiet and clean. The receptionist was cheerfully flirting on the phone when we approached. "One second? ... What's the emergency?"

"Our mother and sister. Phelisa and Precious Battle were brought here with gunshot wounds."

"They're both in surgery." She was sympathetic. "Visitation is over. ... But wait. ..." She fanned an orderly over. "Show them to the waiting lounge on the ninth floor. I'll call Nurse Pottier and let her know you're coming. Just follow him please."

Nurse Pottier was from our neighborhood. She greeted us with hugs and tears. "Pray, just pray."

After five and a half hours of waiting, a middle-aged doctor entered the lounge. He seemed annoyed or exhausted. There wasn't any compassion in his tone as he searched the pages of a file to find Shey's name. "Mr. Mobley was DOA. There wasn't anything we could do. We've done everything possible for Mrs. Phelisa Battle, but the bullet is enlarged too deep into her brain to remove. I don't expect her to make it through the day."

I wanted to punch him, but I had to console Phoenix. I felt vulnerable, helpless, frustrated. "Can we see them, please?"

Our mother and Precious were both beyond recognition; swollen heads and faces. Both defenseless, hooked to respirators, life support, multi-monitors.

The sounds of the machines, the looks on Phihiem and Pharaoh's faces, the pressure of Phoenix hugging my neck, crying, and the fact that Brooke had turned away. It was surreal, nightmarish. But there was a faint beep of hope; the consistent delicate electronic sound of the heart monitors echoed in my ears. That pulse kept me from breaking down, helped me to keep my senses.

The doctor returned with a woman in a skirt suit. "That's them." Again, the tone of the doctor was dry, impersonal.

The female was a little more corrigible, at least she was smiling. "Phelisa Battle was your mother?"

"Mrs. Phelisa Battle is our mother! Who are you?"

"I'm a social worker. Ms. Hicks is my name. If you guys would come with me."

"Excuse me? What is your purpose here?"

"I'm a county official and since you all are considered minors by the law of the state of Pennsylvania, and unless you have a legal guardian, I have to take you to a youth facility."

I wasn't normally the outspoken one, my mother and Precious were the mouth pieces. I was the protector. But a bold courage enveloped me as my role of protector took on a new attribute. "I'm going to point it out to you again; our mother isn't dead! So, your service isn't needed."

There I was worried about losing my mother and sister and didn't have a notion my entire family could be snatched. The social worker didn't try to stop us when we left the intensive care unit.

.....

I was addicted to my morning runs. Running was my high, my way of clearing my mind, freeing myself. The sweating was my way of releasing all the toxic pressure of the world. The aching caused by the sprinting up the stairs to the art museum justified my screaming, venting my rage.

When I entered the house I immediately smelled the food burning. Phoenix was trying to cook breakfast, trying to help out by doing what our mother would've done. With a little help breakfast turned out find. Phoenix and my brothers were cleaning the house when I left.

Brooke lived two blocks over from me. Her older sister was beautiful but also a man hater and didn't want Brooke to trust me. She had good reasons; her life experiences with men had embedded the hatred in her.

No hello or hi, just a nasty stare, then she would shout back into the house, still not addressing me, "He's here! He's just using you. Give him the keys. That's all he wants!"

Brooke did her best to ignore her sister, stepping pass her, then kissing me before rolling her eyes at me as she passed over her car keys.

The determination I was exerting during the weight lifting portion of my training, to rack the 405 pounds on the bench press, was more concentrated for my mother and Precious to awaken and get better.

Nubs wouldn't allow me to rack the weight. "You've got another one in you! Don't you rack that shit! Dig! Dig! Don't die on me! Don't you let it beat you! Dig Pee! Dig! It's the twelve-round! Dig!"

I bounced the weight off my chest and struggled, but locked it out, then racked it; screaming while crying on the inside, sweat mixed with tears, but no one else knew.

Nubs was in overdrive my entire session, testing my limits.

.....

I returned home for lunch to find my brothers and Phoenix selling clothes as if everything was normal. I didn't recognize they were coping with the absence of our mother and Precious, the best way they knew how – by trying to keep my mother's store going. I was in protective mode, mad because they had allowed people into the house. "Moms isn't here! What if they would've robbed you and killed you?"

"We can handle ourselves. Here's the money we made!" Pharaoh was angry.

I could tell we were all hurting and worried. "If I'm not here, don't allow anyone in this house. Do you understand me! Let's eat lunch before we go see Moms and Precious."

Four tuna fish sandwiches, four bowls of beans and rice, and a carton of milk - that was my lunch. My brothers wanted at least two sandwiches and two bowls.

"Your eyes are bigger than your stomachs." Phoenix sounded like our mother. "... Food is too expensive to be thrown away. So, you better eat everything you put on your plate."

.....

It was even harder to believe the bluish balloon size, swollen face belonged to our mother. We were speechless, not knowing what to think or what to say. So we stood there with tears in our eyes.

My mother's doctor was making his rounds. His insensitivity was point blank negative. "She probably will not make it through the week."

"You said she wouldn't make it through the day. You were wrong about that, so it's possible, you'll be wrong again. Please be quiet and just show us to our sister's room."

"I'm being realistic with you, so you can make the proper arrangements to notify other family members, so you all won't be separated."

My birthday was eleven months away. I was the closest person to a legal guardian we had, so unless my mother recovered, or he could keep her alive until I turned 18, it wasn't anyone to notify.

Precious had been taken out of ICU and given her own room. She was still highly medicated. Her appearance wasn't any different than our mother's.

"Is Precious gonna wake up?"

"Going to. Yes, she's going to wake up." I answered Phoenix, not allowing the doctor a chance to say a word. My family was fighters, and a fighter needs confidence and encouragement.

The third leg of my daily training routine consisted of hitting the speed bag and body bag for what seemed like hours, then doing foot work drills and jumping rope to Nubs' grueling pace. Everything was by his stop watch.

Between breaks Nubs noticed how I would quickly make sure my brothers were practicing punching the body bag or correctly hitting the speed bag. I had designated Phoenix as their coach. I was responsible for them and didn't want them out of my sight.

We always ended the session with sparring. Nubs was riding me, screaming at me from the ropes, "Stay focused! Two more fights and we qualify for the Olympics. I understand the stress of all this shit but stay focused on the prize. This is your dream. Reach it and it'll take care of you and them."

It was more than boxing, deeper than most realized. Nubs had been disappointed so many times in life he lived life thinking either you're in a fight, coming out of a fight or headed toward a fight.

"Fight! Dig! Dig!"

I mentally teleported me and my sparring partner; we were two warriors, alone in space. He represented all the misery in my life. I threw a fury of body blow; breaking ribs and elbows, punishing my sparring partner, releasing all of my frustration on him, until being pulled away from him. He dropped to his knees while spitting blood. Nubs loved the viciousness.

When we returned home, Brooke was on our stoop, pissed. "You kept my car all day and didn't even call me!"

She had a right to be mad I had been totally inconsiderate.

"I'm sorry. We were at the hospital, then the gym. I'm sorry."

She knew I was being sincere, so she couldn't stay mad. "How's moms and Precious?"

"The same"

"Let me help you cook and put them to bed."

Brooke played wifey; cooking and cleaning. Once my brothers and Phoenix had taken their baths, they went to sleep. The day at the gym had worn them out.

Brooke and I relaxed in my mother's bed; She really didn't want to have sex, "Stop. Two more fights, then we qualify for the Olympics."

"That's a sure thing. The gold is ours."

She'd attached herself; I was her ticket to a better life, with the added bonus that we loved each other.

Before I could nag her more, she'd slipped her hand into my sweats. I laid back to enjoy the show. It wasn't what I expected but I wasn't disappointed. Her hands were soft and gentle, and the warmth of her mouth on me made my toes curl.

 Once she'd drained my stress, she snuggled under me. "Maybe we should rethink the Olympics? I mean, if you turn pro now, we can get married and have the income to raise them properly. We've got to think about what if moms and Precious don't make it."

Brooke had a way of always reminding me, we were getting married. I wanted to but later in life, "Please don't start." Plus, I couldn't accept the notion of my mother and sister not making it.

"You know what? I'm going home."

"I need your car for tomorrow, so we can get back and forth from the hospital."

"You want me to walk home?"

"No. I want you to stay the night, and I'll drop you off before we go to the hospital."

She threw the keys at me, then tried to leave. I quickly put my shoes on and caught her before she could get beyond the stoop. It didn't take much to convince her to stay.

CHAPTER 8
PRECIOUS

Pain awakened me. It felt as if my brain was trying to tear out of my skull. A pounding sensation sent shock waves through my entire body. I opened my eyes totally confused. I heard voices, but the light from directly above my bed had everything blurred.

"Ms. Battle? Ms. Battle?"

I was gagging on the tube down my throat Unconsciously I snatched on it until I'd pulled it out. Once the images started to come into focus, I realized I was in a bed, then a hospital bed.

"Ms. Battle? Ms. Battle? Calm down."

My eyes adjusted more, and I saw the voices belonged to two detectives; a female and male team.

"Ms. Battle did you see the car jackers? Ms. Battle, any information you can give, may help us solve this murder."

My memory clicked in and all I could do was cry.

"Ms. Battle did you know the car jackers?"

I'd been raised on the code of the street and wasn't about to break them by involving the police. My mental pictures of the blood of my mother and Shey's, plus I'd picked up on the trigger word 'murder' the detective had used. I became hysterical. I snatched off the heart monitor, which flat lined. "I didn't see them! Where's my mother? Where's Shey?"

Nurses rushed into the room. I sat up as if to get out of the bed and the pain in my head almost made me black out. I recognized the head nurse, but I couldn't get my words out.

Nurse Pottier noticed my pain and ordered the detectives out.

"I'm afraid I'm going to have to ask you two to leave."

"We have to ask a few more questions."

"Now is not the appropriate time. She's in no condition to answer questions, as you can see."

I grabbed nurse Pottier's hand, begging, "Where's my moms and Shey?"

"Your mother is in the intensive care unit. I sorry, Shey didn't make it."

"No-ooo! No-ooo! No-ooo!" I felt the pain. It was so intense, it was hurting me to cry.

 After the detectives left I laid there for hours, with tears running down the sides of my face, thinking about Shey and my mother. Anger gave me the strength to bear the pain of sitting up and getting out of bed.

It was a burn victim next to my mother's bed, both their heads and half of their faces were wrapped. Revenge became my motivation as I had to read the charts on the beds to make sure it was my mother. Her hand was limp and cold. I cried and kissed it. I felt responsible.

I had made Shey buy that car. I knew he was making his last drop, I should had waited with my mother until he'd returned.

"I promise you mama; I will get every last one of them. I promise you, if it's the last thing in my life that I do; I'm going to get them."

I had a strong idea of who they were. Only a few people in Philly referred to each other as MO; the members of the study hall.

A nurse spotted me in the ICU, then escorted me back to my bed.

....

Seven days had passed. Shey's estranged aunt had appeared out of nowhere and taken Shey's chronically ill grandfather out of the nursing home and buried Shey in a private ceremony. The only reason she'd did it was to be legal guardian of her father's $200,000 trust fund, Shey had set up to paid the nursing home to provide the best care to his bed ridden grandfather. She'd also transferred her name onto Shey's promotion business accounts. She didn't know about Shey's houses or vehicles, so they went untouched. I received the information from Shey's aunt's lawyer while I was still in the hospital.

.....

After sixteen days I couldn't take the hospital another moment. The doctor was changing the bandage on my head. I hadn't built up the nerves to look at myself in the mirror. I just couldn't.

"The entry wound is just below your hair line and the exit wound. ... Once your hair grows back you can easily cover the entry and the exit wounds..." The mean mug I was giving, made him uneasy, "... Ms. Battle, you're lucky to be alive. The swelling will go down, and eventually your hair will grow back. Since you're refusing to stay any longer at the hospital, please take your medication and get plenty of rest."

My brothers and sister were there to take me home, plus showing their love and support. Phoenix's teary eyes were fixated on my bald head.

"I don't know, it hasn't gone down in all these years. I don't know. Just tell me it can't get any bigger!" Prince's humor was appreciated, but Phoenix instantly smacked the back of Prince's head, then ran to me for protection when Prince reached for her. The warmth of her love was needed.

Prince had brought me the latest, top of the line gear to wear home with an extra touch to kick it off; a fly scarf that matched. He wrapped it over the bandage on my head, and I cried in his arms. "You're still beautiful. Can't anything stop us."

.....

As the days passed I became angrier, mad at everyone for trying to baby me. I hated feeling weak. I didn't want to depend on anyone. Really, I was mad at myself, because I wanted to make it up to my mother and Shey. I was too ashamed to visit my mother's bedside. I wanted to be left alone, but at the same time I hated being alone. I was miserable and confused.

I'd snapped but didn't come apart. The years of studying my mother, my brother and Shey registered; if you're not smart enough to figure it out, find someone who is. If you're not strong enough to handle it, find someone who so. The bottom line was to solve the problem.

I went to one of the neighborhood pool halls in search of my answers; Chub and West, two huge friends of my mother and Shey's. They were enforcers or collectors. They were happy to see I was alive. They both were slow dragging on their bottles of beer. I could tell they were in need of money.

"I need your help." I kept eye contact and my words were clear. "I know who did this."

"Enough said. We can do this now."

"Not tonight, but soon." I had to narrow down the suspects.

"Whenever, whoever. Just call."

"Soon."

.....

I took a cab to one of Shey's houses. A rush of emotions came over me when I entered. His essence was in the air, and I breathed him in, fueling my search. I hadn't quite mastered Shey's ideology, but I knew in the manner he thought. I found guns, and the keys to his big boy SUV. I had to pull over to the side of the road, because my vision became blurred.

.....

I couldn't sleep. I kept reliving the carjacking. My heart and head were pounding.

I stood in the door way of my mother's bedroom for 30 minutes, watching Prince sleep, deciding whether or not to tell him what I knew.

He rolled over a little mad and grouchy, then quickly sat up. "What's what?"

"I know who did this."

"Shey brought this to us"

I wasn't ready for his response. It sent me over the edge. "Someone from your fuckin' study hall did this shit! I've hired Chub and

West. We're going to handle it as soon as I narrow it down.

"How do you know?"

"Who else call each other MO?" He hesitated, thinking instead of reacting. It pissed me off. "Shey tried to give them the shit! They killed him because he didn't have any cash! Grow a dick muthafucka and be a man! What about me and mama? Mama could die because of them! How are you going to look at them the same?"

I knew my brother wasn't a punk. He'd demonstrated that in the ring, but his reaction surprised me when he got out of bed and began to get dressed.

"If we're going to handle it, now is the perfect time."

Up close, my brother's beast mode was different than most; he was calm and precise.

Phoenix and our baby brothers were asleep as we went out the back to meet West and Chub who were waiting in a stolen car.

My brother exposed himself, going to his stash spot in the backyard, grabbing a duffle bag before getting into the car. He then gave directions. None of us asked how he knew, who and where, but he read my stare. "It's a safe haven."

My mind was still wandering as I watched my brother empty out the duffle bag on the back seat. A vest, an Ak47, and two 9mm's with several clips. His calmness was scary. Our eyes locked and he tossed me the vest. No words. By the way he checked the clip and loaded it in the AK 47, I could tell he knew what he was doing.

My weapon of choice was a 9mm. Shey and I had gone to the gun range every other weekend.

Chub, West and Prince put on masks outside of the apartment. I didn't, I wanted whoever was inside to know it was me.

Prince gave a rhythmic knock on the door, which opened. Prince then put the nozzle of the chopper to the nose of one of his closest friends.

"Back up and you might live."

I was right behind West and Chub as we charged into the room, blasting, killing everyone and everything, including their dog. All four of the guys in the apartment were friends of Prince, had been to my mother's house.

West and Chub did a quick search of the pockets and the cabinets, to only find four thousand dollars.

"Where's the goddamn money!" Snatching the guy around that Prince had at gun point.

The guy fell to the floor at my feet, "Where's the cash?"

"That's it!" His eyes and voice pleading. "That's all we've got!" His voice triggered the carjacking memories. He was the one at Shey's window. The one that had shot Shey.

"Imagine that!" I gave him a quick one to the head.

.....

Revenge hadn't filled my emptiness. The void and pain were still there, even though my headaches had become milder. My days were lonely.

My brothers and Phoenix stayed at the hospital and the gym. I occupied my time with the household chores and selling the clothes, which quickly started to empty out.

I had the money to re-up, but none of the boosters were coming by. Eventually I took it on my own to find the boosters my mother was accustomed to using.

"What's what? ... Why haven't you guys brought the shit to the house? I've got money."

"Ray told everyone, he was taking over for Phelisa."

I went directly to Ray's. He was a very coy homosexual. So, he was expecting me when I entered his home, also a store. "I'm sorry about your mother dear. You look just like her. She and I started out together. ..."

I didn't appreciate the fact he was treating me like a child, instead of his equal or superior. I calmly waited until his customers left. The entire bottom level of his home was an upscale clothing store. He approached me and I politely drew my pistol from my purse.

He actually laughed. "Just like your mama. But I know you're smart enough to know it ain't worth killing me. If you can afford to pay them more, they'll beat down your door with clothes. If not, wait your turn. Just like your mother and I waited. ... Child, you're rocking the hell out of that scarf and outfit. I know I've got something you'll love, and it's on me this time."

I wanted to, but he was right; it wasn't worth killing him. I liked the fact he had good taste and the courage to do and be himself. I left and went to each one of Shey's houses, finding guns and ten thousand-dollar stacks of cash hidden throughout the houses. I mentally became Shey. I even found his coded handbook with drawings and incoherent sentences. Trying to figure it out gave me a headache.

I had returned home and given up on trying to decipher Shey's hand book. My medication made me drowsy, but I couldn't take a nap because the television in the den was echoing throughout the house.

"Pharaoh! Phoenix! One of you guys turn down the television, please!"

Nothing changed. Shouting was more painful than the noise from the television. I was pissed. I thought they were ignoring me, but no one was in the den or the house but me. The television was on the history channel. Hieroglyphics were being discussed; pictures like the ones in Shey's handbook. By the time I'd returned with the hand book the program had gone off.

Prince had been complaining about me driving, really, he didn't want me driving Shey's vehicles. He believed it would bring the wrong type of attention. I didn't give a damn what people thought, so I drove it to the library, where I went online and translated the symbols to names. But the sentences were racking my brain.

'You know how he thinks. If it seems complicated, it must be simple.' I analyzed the words, replaced them with synonyms and antonyms. Nothing made sense. Then I realized all the sentences except one, were seven-word sentences. It was simple, but it had to mean something; what, I couldn't figure it out.

"The library is closing." The librarian was polite, but she'd touched me, plus I was frustrated and determined to decode the messages. My expression made her apologize. "I'm sorry if I startled you, but the library is closing."

On my way home, I called to see what Phoenix and the guys would like for dinner, since I hadn't cooked. As I was entering the seven numbers of my home, I realized there were alphabets assigned to the numbers. I could hear Prince's voice, pissed. "Why didn't you cook before you left?"

"What do you want to eat?"

"I cooked already!"

"Good. Bye." I hung up. I didn't feel like being preached to, my mind was on translating the sentences into telephone numbers.

I felt good about my accomplishment; it meant that Shey and I did share a closeness that was more than sex.

The ten-word sentence was a number in New York City, and the symbol represented a thin old man, meaning Flacco.

Prince was still upset when I arrived home. "We all have to pitch in to make this work.”

“I'm doing my part!" I lost my composure but regained it, then backed down, realizing the pressure of responsibility was weighing on both of us.

We both were quiet while we ate as a family. Prince finished first and started spitting orders. He'd deemed himself head of the house.

"Precious, do the dishes.” Then left, like it was law.

"Pharaoh do the dishes.”

"He told you!"

"And I'm telling you.”

Pharaoh was bigger than me, but knew I was meaner, plus our mother had drilled into my brothers to only protect and respect women.

Prince was writing checks for the bills when I entered my mother's bedroom. I was being nosey, but really thinking of a way to express what I had planned.

The checks and bills were equal except the hospital bill.

"I've got a way to make enough money to pay the hospital bill and to start a trust fund for all of us." He stared quietly listening to me. "... If we take over Shey's clientele. ..."

Prince's entire demeanor changed. "That's what got us into this Mess!"

"You're a bitch! A scary ass hoe!"

His movement was so fast and swift and unexpected, that it scared me when he grabbed me.

"If something happens to us, then what? Who's going to look after them? The state? Foster homes!" Referring to my brothers and Phoenix who were in the door way.

I snatched away from him. "Don't you put your hands on me again! ... When we get to far behind on the hospital bill, then what? You think they're going to take care of mama for free?"

"I'm going to apply for Medicare. Nurse Pottier said moms should be eligible."

"You're going to apply for welfare?" My pride, my upbringing, our upbringing went against asking others for help. Others asked us for help, but we helped ourselves. Our mother had instilled that in us. "We don't need to do that!"

"Don't bring that death around us!"

CHAPTER 9

PRINCE

Firmness, promptness. I was forced to come to a compromise, because my better judgement conflicted with my pride. I had to swallow my ego to hand the clerk, the particle payment of my mother's hospital bill. Certain things, situations take priority, and what's usually the most important seems meaningless.

"Does Mrs. Battle have any type of insurance?"

I only shook my head. The receptionist's silence, the pity in her eyes, said more than any words could have. The significance of the expression stayed with me.

I was punishing the speed bag at the gym, zoned out in my own world. Nubs came out of his office, in his usual extremely over intense self, "Damn that pretty shit! Get your ass on the body bag! Make a muthafucka shit his draws! ..." He took control, holding the body bag. "... Hit it! Hit it! Boy Phoenix can hit harder than that!"

He had me beating the body bag the entire third leg of my routine.

.....

Thoughts of my mother's health, my family's financial situation, Precious stupidity, future circumstances under what if; all were present in my mind as I silently cleaned up the back row of the locker room.

Others entered the locker room, unaware of me and even though they were whispering I could hear their conversation, "What are we going to do with that dye shit? It's not coming out."

"I really don't want to burn it. It's too much."

I was far from being green, plus I kept up with the local news and what was happening in the streets. The bank licks were a hot topic, along with a recent home invasion, that left five dead.

I purposely hit the mop bucket against the lockers, making my presence known. Ra and Melik peeped at me before all five men left the room. I knew them all. Ra and Melik instructed study sessions, and they all were ushers; distinguished, well groomed, soldier types, in excellent physical shape to be in their forties.

.....

School was only days away. I'd taken Phoenix and my brothers shopping, basically window shopping, because I was only buying everyone new shoes. They wanted new clothes, but our gear was practically brand new, so we didn't need clothes. They were somewhat disappointed. I understood the peer pressure to have the latest, most popular name brand, but bills had to be paid. My mother had soiled us, to keep us happy.

.....

I hadn't understood why people looked at my family differently, we were from the hood, so I'd assumed all were the same to a various of degree. But once we arrived at the County building, the explicit disparity explained itself. The depressed, the destitute, the disarrayed and the disgusted. Their posture, their entire personas were alien to my family.

We were there to apply for Medicare for our mother. The case manager was surprised when all four of us entered her office.

"Good afternoon. ... Let me get more chairs."

"It's fine. We'll stand." I really felt more comfortable on my feet.

Phoenix accepted the chair as the case manager passed me back the application.

"Mr. Battle the application has to be completed."

I'd answered the questions as best as I could, with what little medical and financial history I knew about my mother or could legally explain. "I'm afraid that's all the information we have."

"Mr. Battle without the information, we can't determine if your mother qualifies for Medicare. Maybe someone else in your family can complete it?"

We never knew either side of our grandparents, both had died before we were born, and both of our parents were only children. I felt my frustration building. "We are our only family. Unless you want me to make up answers, I can't complete it."

"Unless it's completed I can't help you. Complete the application." She hadn't told me to lie, but it was understood.

She walked me through the questions, estimating at answers that would qualify my mother, which I agreed could be. Once done, the feeling of accomplishment was undone. "You know Medicare only covers a small portion of the bill?"

I was grateful, but dissatisfied.

.....

I couldn't think of anything to better our circumstance. I was becoming desperate. The clothing supply was almost out, the money was drying up, and I was taking it out on my sparring partners; Nubs loved my rage.

"That's good! That's good! Hit the showers!"

Melik and Ra with the three others from the study hall, were finishing their showers as I entered to start mine. No eye contact was made, but everyone was aware of the other.

I was half dressed as Ra and the others were passing to leave out of the locker room.

"MO, I've got the answer to that problem. I couldn't help overhearing."

"What're you talking about?"

"A week ago."

"So you did hear something?"

"Enough."

"So you did?"

It was a threat, and I was in the wrong for putting my nose in someone else business. But I couldn't let the opportunity pass. "If you've solved your problem, then I didn't hear anything. But if you still have that problem, I'm the solution."

Their eyes were sizing me up. They knew my family's history, my character and they had access to me; at home, at the gym and they knew which high school I attended.

"Youngin' what's your answer?"

"A dime on the dollar. That's better than throwing it away or burning it."

"If anything funny comes from this, we're going to burn you." Melik was more muscles than brains.

Ra was the deliberate one, "Youngin' what're you going to do with it?"

"I'm not asking where it came from, and I'll feel more comfortable keeping my business to myself."

Melik stepped forward in an aggressive manner, then stopped once seeing my smirk. He thought twice about it and decided it was better to listen to me.

"... You don't want to do that. Your business is yours and mine is mine. Just tell me how much or you've solved your problem, and everything's forgotten."

Ra eyed me for more than a moment. "Thirty-four hundred. Have it tomorrow night."

Since it was kind of early I dropped Phoenix and my brothers off at home, then returned Brooke's car to her. I was planning on doing some sofa sitting, spend some quality time with her, watching television or just listening to her dream about our tomorrow; plus, I wanted, needed to talk to someone to see if they thought I was making the right decision. Her sister answered the door with a vindictive smirk.

"She ain't here. She's hanging with friends. Gim'me her car keys."

"Tell her. ..." The heifer took the keys and closed the door before I could finish my sentence.

CHAPTER 10
PRECIOUS

Everything I'd been through had formed, molded, helped me develop, gradually producing the impulse, the boldness necessary to fight to continue.

I'd built up the nerves to move out of my mother's house and into one of Shey's houses. I was going to do it; take over Shey's heroin customers regardless of what Prince had warned. I wasn't going to sit around and allow my family to live in poverty.

My nerves froze at the sound of the heavy Latin accent, "... This is Shey's assistant. I'm going to be continuing his operation."

A light-hearted laugh. "Where's Shey?"

"Deceased. He died less than three months ago. I'm his assistant. I need to fill an order of six."

There was a contemplating silence, "If he trusted you enough to give you my information, all right. ..." Details and arrangements were made.

Chub and West weren't hustlers, and didn't understand the meaning of stacking ends, plus they were terrible gamblers, so they were very appreciative of my permanent job offer; to be my muscle.

The pawn shop owner was a close friend of my mother. He didn't have or wouldn't sell me a heroin tester. Chub and West knew of a human tester; Dora who used to also work for Shey at one time. It surprised me, but I wasn't willing to risk exposing myself to anyone if it wasn't absolutely necessary, at the same time I couldn't risk rescheduling with Flacco, so I agreed to use Dora.

I came up with a plan; Once Dora agreed to

be the tester. Chub and West would blind folded Dora in her apartment. They used big shades to cover the blind fold as they led her to the SUV.

"Boss lady, are we ready to hit the road?"

"Yes."

Dora heard my voice, "Thanks for the job. Things been hard with all the jackers out here. What do you want me to call you?" She didn't look like an addict. She had her weight and a glow to her skin. She was actually fly, but she was a functional addict. My mother and Shey had taught me; anyone with a dependency can't be trusted. "... Chub, West. Vouch for my thoroughness. Tell her?"

If they would've said something, it wouldn't have mattered. "Your blind fold and you not knowing my name are safety nets for you and me. I don't have to worry about you telling, and you don't have to worry about me killing you."

It was a silent ride to the suburbs of New York City. The estate of Flacco's house was massive. His muscle met us in the turnabout driveway. Three of them stepped forward as if to pat search us.

"Hell naw! Get the fuck back!"

They were trying us, as if we were pie or green; disarm you, then take your money or your life. The front door opened, and a cocky laughter stepped out in the form of Flacco, sleek and debonair.

"Well, Ms. Shey. We don't have to do business."

"Fine, I didn't like making this long ass ride anyway. I guarantee you someone in Philly will love doing business with me; with the numbers I'm about to generate."

More laughter, but this time it was more genuine, from his gut. He was greedy but smart. "I've got a strange feeling this arrangement is going to get the best of me. C'mon in." Once inside he assumed the position against the wall of the immaculate house. "Ms. Shey, pat search me. Only you and I are going into my study."

I searched his slim but firm body, "My tester will accompany us."

"My turn ladies." His touch made my flesh crawl.

Inside the study the walls were covered with medieval memorabilia; swords, battle axes, shields.

I had to stop Dora from removing the blind fold. "Don't forget what I said."

Flacco was very observant. "He taught you well. Trust no one. Shey was like a son to me. This Is nine. Bring back my money for the extras. This is where he topped off every two weeks."

I whispered so only Dora could hear. "Are you going to shoot it or snort it?"

"Just put a bump in my hand, and I'll tell you the quality of it in 15 seconds."

I and Flacco both watched in awe as Dora pulled her skirt to the side and massaged the small pebble size piece of heroin in her vagina. She immediately grabbed for anything in reach; my arm and took hold with both hands, trembling, standing on her tip toes, sighing, then almost collapsing.

"Oh shit! You can step on this twice and it still might be too strong."

Flacco was eyeing the milky white orgasmic substance running down the insides of Dora's legs. It was perverted, and he was a pervert.

I pressed the send button on my cell, then a knock came at the door; West with the backpack of money. I disgustedly exchanged Dora for the money, then dumped the cash on Flacco's desk. A female entered and began counting the money, then was about to weigh the kilos of heroine.

"That's not necessary."

"You trust me?"

"No. If they're short, I'm going to take it out of the three. So, it's your lost."

.....

I recognized my reflection in the rearview mirror, but not my eyes they'd turned cold, relentless. I was punishing myself; taking penitentiary chances, death defying risks. I wasn't afraid of death. I was craving it in a sick twisted way, justifying it as for the good of my family. I was alone, the feeling twas eating at me. I wanted the support of my family. They had always been my safety net. But I couldn't take the chance of anything happening to them on my account again. If I'd listened to Prince and Shey the first time, my mother wouldn't be fighting for her life. It was my fault, and there I was again determined to defy Prince and Shey.

I removed my scarf. My hair had grown long enough to cover my scars. Angry tears warmed my face. Not vanity; I wanted to see my reminders, my motivation. I drove to the local barber shop in our community; my brothers had been getting their haircuts there their entire lives. Their barber was hesitant about cutting my hair into a bald fade, until I went into my super diva mode.

"I'm pretty confident in my beauty. I don't need to hide behind hair."

The owner had a thing for my mother, but he was too fly for his own good. All eyes were on me when my new barber brushed the last of the dead hairs off me.

I approached the owner. "Can I have a word with you please, outside?" He followed and listened. "... I'm going to prepay for my brothers' haircuts for a year. But I want you to tell Prince, the free haircuts are your way of sponsoring him." Once I placed five hundred dollars in his hand, he understood exactly what I was saying.

I did the same thing with the local grocery store manager and the sporting goods store; prepaid accounts disguised as sponsorship.

I went to Beckon's clothing manufactory and waited for an hour. The owner, Cuda Bay, my brother's so-called mentor, but most others were calling him the rebirth of Malcom X. His male receptionists escorted me into his office.

Cuda Bay had been informed of my request and was somewhat hesitant. "Ms. Battle, how do you make a living?"

I ignored his question. "This is a way for me to promote my brother and help a Black owned business. There's nothing illegal about this. In actuality; your company should've approached my brother, being he's a member of your study hall and resides within this community."

We negotiated a partnership and finally agreed on the terms.

I was tough but still a woman. Shopping is and was a relief for me. I ended up shopping more for my brothers and sister than myself. With Prince penny pinching, I knew he hadn't bought back to school clothes and I didn't like the idea of them wearing last year gear.

No one was at the house, so I neatly put the clothes into my brothers and sister's drawers and left. I felt good, so I went to the hospital and arranged for the gift store to deliver fresh flowers daily to my mother's rooms.

I ran into a little difficulty at the administration office with paying cash.

"... Muthafucka, what does it matter if I slung pussy, sucked dicks, pleaded, begged or prayed for this money?" The twenty grand I paid seemed irrelevant when I read the remaining balance. "... Goddamnit!"

I was ashamed, but I'd built up the nerves to deliver some flowers to my mother's room, but when I got close enough to the room I could hear the voices of my brothers and sister. I didn't want to face them. I backed back to the elevator. A nurse exited, and I gave her the flowers, "Will you please deliver this to Mrs. Phelisa Battle, please?" I pressed the button and the doors were closing before she'd answered.

.....

A phone call. A distorted voice. Direction to another phone. Orders were received, and directions given. Instructions followed; a dumpster for the drop of the backpack of money. A gift-wrapped box on one end of a bench with an old lady on the other end feeding the birds.

"Is this for me?"

"Is it?"

The fellow, unknowingly was being followed by West while Chub retrieved the money, then returned to the SUV to me, where I counted the amount before calling off West. I used the distorted voice to finalize the deal with the fellow, "Thank you."

"Hey! What if I need to contact you tomorrow?"

"I'll contact you daily."

I used the same discretion with all of my clients.

CHAPTER 11

PRINCE

Running: I would be lost in my own world, my escape from it all. Everything on the streets seemed abandoned, deserted. I would run faster, trying to leave it all. Sprinting towards the break of dawn, knowing if I made it to the next day there was a chance. The sunshine and the people began to appear. Somber faces, tired, fed up with the same routine, day in and day out. But there was always an encouraging nod, a smirk fostering to continue running.

By the time I'd finished my shower, Phoenix would be up trying to prepare breakfast. Since Precious had moved out, Phoenix had begun trying to do the things our mother would've.

"Go get dressed, and wake up your brothers. I've got this."

We all were excited about the first day of school. All three of them strutted into the kitchen with brand new clothes on.

"Prince we need haircuts."

"I want to cut my hair too."

I ignored Phoenix, "We're going get them on Saturday."

"What about me?"

"I like long hair on females, plus yours is too pretty to cut. Did mom buy that for you guys?"

"I don't know. It was in my drawers."

Phoenix and Phihiem both had dumbfound expressions, so I couldn't tell if Pharaoh was lying.

"If you guys are stealing, I swear I'm going to put hands on all three of you!"

"Mann, we haven't stolen anything."

"They were in our drawers, like he said." Phoenix would never lie to me under any circumstances.

"Sit down and eat your breakfast, so we'll be ready to leave when Brooke gets here."

We waited around on Brooke as long as possible, then I walked two blocks to the elementary school Phoenix attended and the middle school Pharaoh and Phihiem went to, which were deeper into our hood.

Phoenix's principal was once my second-grade teacher and the reason I enjoyed learning. He was also the only Black male teacher I'd had in school. We both had mutual respect for one another and always greeted each other with firm handshakes and smiles.

My grades had given me the good fortune to attend a private high school, which like Saint Mary's hospital, was on the border of Philly, and had been forced by the city to accept at least 25 inner city students on scholarship, a year. The grounds of Saint Mary's High School were the size of a college campus with all the amenities.

Brooke was also a scholarship recipient. She spotted me when I entered the building. The way she approached I could tell she was pissed, highly upset.

"I'm the one who had to take a bus to school. Why are you pissed?"

"You drove around with my emergency brake up! Now my brakes and the drums have to be replaced!"

"Your brakes were fine when I returned your car. Your sister had to have driven it like that. ... Where were you last night, anyway?"

"I was at the library, then I hung out with Sasha. Don't change the subject. The repair work is going to cost $375. I only have $75. Can you help?"

"All I have is enough for the mortgage, but if you can wait ..."

I was about to tell her my plan but she cut me off. "Damn Prince. Every time I ask you for anything, it's wait, wait, wait! When you want some, do I tell you to wait?" I couldn't say a word, she was right. "I love you Pee. Do you love me?"

"Yeah, but what does this have to do with $300? I mean ..."

"If you turn pro, we wouldn't have to worry about money. We ..."

It was too early for so much drama. "Stop it. I've got class."

"All right! All right!" She was infuriated by my walking off.

My first period was advance chemistry. After the instructor lectured on his syllabus of the course and his requirements, he suggested, "... I recommend you form study groups no larger than six students."

I started to sign up, but I couldn't commit because my schedule was too hectic.

"You're not going to join us?"

I had noticed Campbell several times over the last three years, a very pretty girl with defined facial features, so profound it was hard to believe she was white.

"I don't have the time."

I noticed her again on the crowded transit bus after school. She had her face in a book, seated next to an elderly lady.

As we rode along, the community, the streets smoother, the yards bigger, the grass richer, it was foreign compared to Philly.

I watched how politely Campbell exited the bus.

Saint Mary's hospital was less than ten minutes from the high school. My mother was still in a coma. I took her hand as I sat beside her. I wanted her strength, I wanted her to wake up, so I wouldn't have to take the risks to provide for the family. It was different than doing something that was bad but good for the community. There was no predator to eliminate. I would be the one taking a chance of being eliminated, taken away from the responsibility my mother had bestowed upon me, 'Prince, take care of my babies.'

.....

It was a negative action or no action; like when you realize you're falling, you automatically reach out to grab whatever to help you catch your balance or to stop the falling.

Melik and Ra approached me in the locker room with a backpack. "You're ready?"

"I'm short $400. You can take four stacks out and everything's everything."

"Youngin' you'll take all of it or none of it. You owe us"

Nubs was standing by the exit as Ra and Melik left out. Once Nubs and I made eye contact. I saw his concern.

"Kid, you've worked hard for this. It's in reach. Don't jack it off by being stupid."

"Everything's clean. I'm out."

.....

Since Brooke's car was down. I had to walk. I recognized the stares and the acknowledgments. When I got to Brooke's block, I had to stop once seeing Brooke hugging and kissing a guy on the side of a new car in front of her home. Instead of confronting her, I turned around. I was hurt; mentally and emotionally. My heart was broken. The only experience I'd had with being hurt was in the ring, so I used the lessons learned in the ring to help me deal with it; take a knee, gather yourself, find composure, control your reactions, be poised until you're ready for confrontation.

I entered my home to loud music, and dirty dishes were in the sink and on the table.

"Pharaoh! Phihiem! Phoenix!" My brothers came running. "Just because mom isn't here doesn't mean we live like pigs! This is our home! Have some pride in it! Now clean up this mess!"

Phoenix entered the kitchen dressed in a too big house robe and a shower cap, "I told them to clean up this mess while I took my bath. But they told me to shut up! Talk now!"

"You're snitching now? Huh? Stop laughing. There's nothing funny. She told you right. Now clean up this mess."

They cleaned up while I ate.

"Yo. Hold up. Where's your homework?" The guys went to get theirs while Phoenix sat there smiling at me.

"You're going to be a good daddy one day."

"When I said let me see your homework, that meant you too. Go get your homework for me to see."

"My homework is to read a chapter of the book I checked out from the school library about boxing."

Later that night Phoenix came into my mother's bedroom with the book. "I need your help with this word please?"

I knew she didn't want to sleep alone. "Let me see," making room for her in the bed. "... pe-er-fer-el, peripheral vision. You can read to me until I fall asleep but wake me up when you leave."

The alarm clock went off at 1:30 AM. Phoenix was stretched out in a deep sleep next to me. I snuck out of bed without awakening her.

I took the backpack of dye money and one of my brother's bicycles. I rode all over town cashing in the dye money at coin exchange machines; car washes, anywhere I could find a coin machine. I would put on my snap on mask just in case there were surveillance cameras. I returned home at 4:30 AM, loaded with coins. I tried to rest but Phoenix woke me up at six o'clock, screaming. "You missed your morning run!"

"I've done it already. Go wake up your brothers and tell them their room better be clean by the time I finish cooking."

Life was clouded with pain. Some say a mistake can be corrected but there wasn't anything that could erase the pain.

I was emptying my locker when Brooke approached extra cheerful. I had thoughts of cramming her into the locker.

"Here. This's the ends you needed."

"I don't need it. What do you need all your books for?"

"How did you get the money?" Her silence brought back something my mother had told me; it's going to be a lot of fast, nothing ass heifers trying to use their stuff to get what they can out of you. So, make all of them earn your trust; because love doesn't happen overnight.

I knew Brooke viewed me as a meal ticket, but I also thought she had loved me.

"Don't worry. I saw how. I came by with this last night." I controlled my rage, but I threw the money in her face.

She was dumbfounded at first, then realized that we were over, and the tears started. I didn't wait for an explanation. She had to stop to pick up the money before the others tried too.

I couldn't study. It took half of my chemistry test to get focused. I was last to finish.

.....

The withering flowers in my mother's hospital room was reminiscent of life. Since our financial situation had improved I bought new flowers for my mother and threw out the old ones.

My mother's skin and lips seemed so dry, that I put my books aside, then put lotion on her entire body. My mother was shriveling. I wanted to cry. "I, we need you mom. Don't leave us, please?"

On the other corner of the block from the gym was a liquor store, a pawn shop, and the check cashing joint I used to cash the coins in for money orders and $600 cash. The clerk was flirtation at first, then became pissed once seeing she had to count coins.

As soon as I entered the gym, RA followed me to my locker. I gave him a half hug with a shake, hiding the fact I'd put the $600 knot into his hand. No words, but his eyes showed he was puzzled as he backed away.

It wasn't his business, so I didn't explain how. I let him kept wondering.

.....

My release, my moment to vent, to pour my punishment back onto the world was when I was sparring. I had three sparring partners, neither lasted an entire around. Ribs breaking, elbows splintering and mouth pieces flew out of their mouths – Nubs enjoyed every moment of it.

"Nice work! Nice muthafuckin' work kid! They'll be all right. That's what they're getting paid for. Hit the showers kid." Calming me down like a pit bull being taken out of the pit.

.....

When I arrived home. the house was clean and Phoenix, Pharaoh and Phihiem's homework were on the table next to the slow cooker. I still punched them with gut checks.

"That's for not doing your push-ups and sit-ups. Then I faked a gut check on Phoenix who pivoted and gut checked me.

"You've got to be ready!"

I fell to the floor, acting hurt, then started tickling Phoenix. She loved the affection. My brothers came to her defense, tickling me. I had all three pinned, tickling them and laughing with them. We all needed the love.

I ignored Brooke's calls, but wished I had her car while riding the bike over the city, exchanging the dye money for coins. It took me a whole week before all the dye money was gone.

.....

Unexpected gifts are the best. My chemistry instructor posted the test scores as the bell rang. The entire class was trying to read the list. I was able to see over the crowd. It looked like my name was second on the list. To make sure I had to move closer. It wasn't intentionally done, but I was leaning against Campbell's behind. She was actually tall for a woman. With her in the position of leaning forward our bodies were a perfect fit.

From the moment I touched Campbell, I realized I was in violation, but her sensuousness held me. She was so soft, it felt as if she was melting. I inhaled the berry scent of her hair and became hungry for more. She shot me an elbow, that stunned me, then turned around mad with an attitude.

"You!" She was pissed to the point of punches, which I playfully slapped down while backing up apologizing.

"I was only trying to see my grade. I'm sorry. I didn't know you were working with all of that." The more I laughed the harder she tried to hit me. "Don't be mad at me, because I scored higher than you."

She stopped and turned up her nose, then walked away.

Precious met me in the hallway. My sister has always been a stuntter, and I've always been her big brother that ran boys away. So, the stares she was getting, I was giving back to the guys walking by.

"Is everything all right at the house? Do you need money for anything?"

"Thank you, but we're straight. How about you? You're taking your medicine?"

"Yes. What did the doctor say about mom?"

"I'm meeting with him this evening. Everything is straight, right? We've got classes to attend." I could tell she was stalling, wanted something.

"I'm taking Friday off to be at your fight. Phoenix and the guys can ride with me? So, they won't miss the fight." Her eyes were begging.

I loved my sister and would've done anything for her. "If you're done with your business. But if not, you know the answer. We love you but I'm not putting them in harm's way by allowing them to be with you."

She was furious but allowed me to kiss her forehead before I headed off to class.

.....

Since I went to a private school, there was no such thing as school busses. So the students from Philly without cars and the school employees without cars used the transit busses. I was playing the background, watching Campbell, while waiting on the bus to take me to the hospital.

Campbell entered the bus and quickly started back studying. I realized she hadn't signaled for her usual stop, which was quickly approaching, so I pressed the button.

"Campbell, Campbell! This is your exit."

"Thank you," Hurrying to gather her things, then realized it was me. Her smile turned to a frown as she left the bus.

There were new flowers in my mother's hospital room, beside the ones I'd bought a day earlier.

"I see Precious came by. I hope you two had a long talk. She won't listen to me." I continued my one-sided conversation while putting lotion on my mother's body. "I won't be here tomorrow. Tomorrow's my big fight. Then one more, and our dream comes true. We'll qualify for the Olympics." I'd taken my mother's hand, but when I tried to release it her grip held tight, then relaxed. It scared me so that I took my mother's hand again and felt the warmth of her grip. I almost broke the button that summoned the nurse. Her doctor came along with nurse Pottier.

"She grabbed my hand! Look!"

The doctor's expression didn't change. He checked my mother's vital signs, then took my joy. "It's a sign of deterioration. I hate to sound so bleak, but your mother will never recover. I'm sorry. She has very little brain activity."

He was mechanical and heartless but was smart enough to leave the room once seeing the sadness and anger in my eyes.

.....

Each punch that hit the body bag had as much power as my thoughts of life for myself and my brothers and sisters without our mother.

Ra came over and grabbed the bag, whispering, "Do you have five grand yet?" My blows to the body bag almost knocked him down, "If you do, bring it to the hall tomorrow."

"I have a fight out of town tomorrow."

Nubs screamed from across the gym, "Ra, get, get your ass away from him! You don't know a damn thing about boxing! Talk that soul brother shit to him later! Get your ass over there and lift some weights with the rest of them fake ass Black panthers!"

Ra nodded to me, then left before Nubs got there. Nubs took control of the bag, still gritting in Ra's direction.

"Boxing is a sport. Leave the politics to the politicians. At least until after the Olympics. He knew our views differed on social issues, so he quickly changed the topic. "Let's get the sparring over with."

.....

At three in the morning, Nubs was surprised to see Pharaoh, Phihiem and Phoenix come out of the house with me. I hadn't had a fight without them being there, and I wasn't about to have one. "Where are they going?"

"With you." Phoenix answered with an expression like wasn't it obvious, holding the van's door open while we put the bags inside.

Nubs hadn't started the van. He was just sitting there staring at me.

"They're my motivation."

"Don't they have school today?"

Once I put my ear buds in and zoned out, Nubs started the van and pulled off.

Phoenix and the guys quickly fell asleep as we rode the open highway. Their trust in me, made them comfortable enough to relax, not worry. They thought the world of me and knew I would do everything in the world for them regardless the weight of it.

The little city in Indiana, looked like Mayberry. A small mining city, that had seen better economic times. Out of the 2,500 residents, not one of color, but they were hospitable; the diner, the gym and the looks from the ladies.

The turnout for the fight was huge. The entire town was in their small civic arena to root for their local fighter; a corn fed, massive redneck, youngster. He came out on the attack from the ringing of the bell. His first punch glazed the corner of my eye and the tip of my nose; a haymaker, a fury of them, but the rest never came close to landing. I side stepped, bobbed, two stepped, then I saw the opening. I came out of my bob and handed a solid upper cut, square on the chin of the youngster, lifting him off his feet. The crowd went silent; amazed and disappointed, then I heard Precious' cheers, her proud supportive cry, broke the silence.

"Hell yeah! That's how you handle it! Hell yeah!"

CHAPTER 12

PRINCE

Motivation starts with desire. Once you acquire the craving no one can stop the drive. Me and my brothers were at the hospital listening to Phoenix rave to our mother about how easy and quick my fight had been.

A lot of the swelling had gone down, so our mother's face was close to normal. She appeared to be sleeping, but Phoenix continued, "Prince has a little bruise but ..."

A nurse entered the room with the equipment to bathe my mother, "Excuse me. It's her bath time. ..."

The thought of someone bathing our mother, the strongest willed person on earth to us, was depressing. Before we could leave the room, the nurse had started. The sight of our mother's limp, almost lifeless body was overwhelmingly disheartening. I could see my brothers and Phoenix's spirits dropping, giving up hope.

The nurse paused when she saw me take my mother's hand.

I felt my mother's weak grip, which stirred my heart and gave me hope. "Feel this! Come feel this!"

It was uplifting, but it didn't change the fact we were still underdogs.

...

Sunday dinners were something my mother took extra pride in. She would fuss to make sure all of us were there. I was trying to prepare a Sunday meal after we returned from the hospital, but my specialty when it came to cooking was breakfast. I'd forgotten to put the sugar in the cornbread. The fried chicken was extra crispy, but blood squirted out of a drumstick when Pharaoh bit into it. The cool-aid and rice and beans were good.

"Mama's don't do this?"

"Or taste like this."

I ended up cooking a country breakfast for dinner.

...

Running in the still of the morning always calmed my raging storm, helped me to see how the roads connected.

At school, everyone was excited about me being one victory away from qualifying for the Olympics, as if they were about to qualify. My success was theirs by association; a link, inspiring them to believe anything can be done.

During PE I didn't risk any freak accidents shooting ball or playing flag football, I worked out, lifting weights with linemen from the football team who drove me as hard as Nubs.

I had passed my maxed-out point and entered into uncharted weights. The team members were urging me to keep up with the strongest two linemen on the team. I struggled, but I racked 405 pounds.

"That's it for me. I can't risk hurting my shoulders."

Both linemen were at least 320 pounds, and both were amazed by my strength, "Prince, just between us; are you on that juice?"

"Hell naw!"

"He just ain't getting none, with his match coming. Cock strong ass!"

...

Campbell was eyeing me at the bus stop but hadn't waved or nodded; no type of acknowledgment. But instead of her taking a seat on the bus, she stood, then stopped me when I tried to pass. "Look, if you help me bring my grade up in chemistry, I'll be able to drive my car to school, and I'll drive you to the hospital every day after school? This test is a third of our six-week grade. ..." She was close enough that I could smell the mint in her mouth, "... Ooh, whoa! The blog said your fight was a one hitter quitter."

There was a little swelling and a raspberry on the corner of my nose and eye.

"He actually missed."

"Whoa. A good thing for you."

"Yeah, but a very bad thing for him."

Unconsciously she was touching my face, examining the bruise, then realized how intimately close we were. "I'm sorry."

"It's all right. I'll help you, but I might every once and awhile need a favor."

The grimace on her face and the hard shake of her head showed her disgust and disapproval, "I'm not a groupie!"

"Not like that! I'm training anyway. Get your head out of the gutter. What's giving you a hard time?"

"The properties."

"Wait, you made an 86 on the last examine."

"Yes, but I need to raise my overall GPA to guarantee I get accepted to Yale. So I want to make straight A's."

I was impressed; Beautiful with a brain. The bus jerked, and we became belly to belly. "Call me tonight about 9:15, and I'll solve your problem. Here. This is your stop."

She accepted my phone number, still suspiciously staring at me.

...

I'd used the last of the lotion mixed with my mother's favorite perfume, moisturizing my mother's skin. The scent had engulfed the entire room. I was gathering my books from studying, about to leave when her doctor and two suits entered.

"Mr. Battle, I'm glad we didn't miss you. Allow me to introduce you to Dr. Win, one of the world's leading neurologist."

I was skeptical of why the change of heart by a doctor that was so positive my mother wouldn't live or recover. "Has my mother's condition improved?"

"No, but the research of her condition could help all of mankind. Your mother's health is deteriorating. Within a year, she'll be braindead."

I'd taken all the negativity I could stand from the doctor, so I gut checked him with a super hard hook. He dropped to all fours, vomiting everything that was in his stomach. Dr. Win stepped back, but the other suit, the director of administration stayed calm, "Mr. Battle, we know this is a sensitive matter. But the corporation that Dr. Win represents will cover all financial obligations plus provide trust funds for you, your brothers and your sisters. There's time to think about it. Excuse our interruption."

They were asking me to donate my mother's brain, life to science. Regardless of any facts, I couldn't; not if I wanted to keep my promise to take care of her children.

My determination to keep my promise and my frustration from being uncertain of what to do, were changing me. I was mad and mean.

At the gym, Ra spotted me at the water cooler, then came over.

I didn't see any need for small talk, "Did you find that in your locker?"

I'd placed the five grand there.

"Yes. Where do you want me to put yours?"

"Just leave it in your locker."

"I don't like the idea of you going in and out of my locker."

"Alright. Just don't think about it."

"Youngin' stop trying me."

I didn't want to take any risk that could take me away from my brothers and sisters, but I need the fifty-grand. I understood the press at the hospital was because of money or the lack of money. The whole situation was suffocating, stifling, caused me to resort to the only means I had to get the cash.

CHAPTER 13

PRECIOUS

My entire life my mother had told me how unique and special I was, building my belief in myself. So, when others treated me different or said I thought I was better than them it was true. I had been reading since I was five. My mother, while we would wait for people to stop by to buy clothes, would read to me, then made me repeat the words as she pointed to them. On top of that, math was a given in our household. My mother had my confidence so high, that for the majority of time, she was my only friend, the only person that wasn't jealous and envious of me.

Being a loner at school wasn't bad. It actually made me more popular; people wanted to know more about me, tried to befriend me. Rumors and lies stayed in the air about me. I'd only had one best friend besides my mother and Shey. It was June, and the friendship ended the moment I started my freshman year of high school; I was never a follower.

I realized June had become a part of the in-crowd instead of a trend setter. June was pretty and smart, but her family was extremely broke, so money impressed her and obsessed her. She was a grade ahead of me and a scholarship recipient at Saint Mary's as well. We acknowledged one another, but that had been the extent to our relationship. So it surprised me when June and a group of super uppity senior girls approached me in the hallway at school, "Can we have a moment with you?"

"Why?"

"We want your help. Just a good word with some of your connects."

"What?"

"So we can promote fundraisers for the senior class trip."

Some of the girls in front of me were the ones who had started most of the rumors and lies. "Why should I help you?"

"Your brother is a senior! It's for a good cause."

I understood June was indirectly referring to the income of my household and most of the wannabe girls in front of me, being from the hood, and in fact, needed the fundraiser so they could continue to play with and pretend to be one of the rich.

"Well, you should ask my brother for my connects." I knew the importance of networking and its value within the promotion business, so I walked off, letting the girls know they were unimportant to me.

Prince was at his new locker, which was near my class. "What's new?"

He looked good with a fresh haircut. He updated me on what our mother's doctor had suggested, and on the wellbeing of my brothers and Phoenix.

I was used to getting second looks from guys and girls, but it bothered me when someone just stopped and stared, gawking.

"Is there a problem with you?"

Prince turned around to see who I was talking too. He realized it was Campbell, standing, waiting in the back ground.

"Don't trip. That's Campbell."

I knew of her, a smart, Kim Kardashian look alike. "I know who she is. What I'm about to find out is, why she's all in my mouth."

"She's my study bubby. She's waiting on me. Chill. ... About dropping ..."

Before he finished his sentence I walked off. I didn't feel like arguing about me spending my money on my brothers and sister, and going in and out of my mother's house when I was ready.

The discussion with June and the fund raiser group helped me figured out how I could cleanly deposit my heroin money.

I was at Saint Mary's public library on a PC, incorporating my promotion business when

I noticed Campbell who was across the room, staring in my direction. Once we made eye contact Campbell immediately stood and approached me. I sized her up; her style, her walk. We were close to the same size. I wasn't really concerned because I had my 9mm in my purse.

"I don't mean to be rude, but I don't want to start any drama between you and Prince. I'm only interested in Prince as a friend. He's helping me raise my average in chemistry."

My brother was the finest man at Saint Mary's High, and the idea of a white tomboy, dissing him, erked me. "My brother couldn't be in to your homely dressing ass anyway."

"What? Who are you to judge me? You don't know me! Queen knockoff!"

I stood at once. Campbell wasn't intimidated. The librarian shushed us.

"White girl, you're lucky I don't have time to whup your ass! And please remember this; There's not a damn thing fake about me or what I wear!"

...

As long as I stayed moving the depression of loneliness wouldn't bother me, but at night alone in the house, regardless of the noise Chub and West made downstairs; playing videogames, my sadness consumed me. My thoughts would have me crying to myself. I'd read; writing your thoughts down was a good therapy. I could never get pass one sentence in my dairy: 'Buy a dog because I need a friend'

Too many thoughts were in my head to sleep, and the stillness of night made me think about the meaningless of life, made me ask myself could death be better.

I would get dressed in the middle of the night and have Chub to just drive me around, so I could sleep until the sun came up.

.....

I hate surprises, always have and always will. That's why I try to plan for every circumstance, and try to predict and stay ahead of change, and when possible create or direct change to my advantage. I was unnerved when my name was announced to report to the principal's office. On my way, I tried to eliminate reasons why; my purse and my 9mm were hidden in the Land Rover, it was no way they could've found it. Thoughts of my mother of my sister and brothers stuck in my mind, so I sped up my pace.

I entered the office without the school secretary announcing me.

Ms. Coffee, our white middle-aged principal and another tacky dressed white woman, the school's psychologist both stopped what seemed to be a pleasant conversation.

"What's wrong? Has something happened with my mother?"

"No-oooo Calm down. This isn't an emergency. Dr. Ashworth has brought to my attention, the stress you and Prince could be enduring. Therapy could be useful." Passing the conversation with a glance at Dr. Ashworth.

"I think it would be wise and beneficial for you and Prince to schedule weekly therapy sessions.

"Excuse me? Have either one of you ever interacted with me or my brother? I have a better question. Would these sessions be mandatory?"

"No. But they're help you deal with the stress."

"What you two fail to understand; is the majority of people that look similar to my brother and me, deal with and has dealt with stress everyday of their lives because stress is a part of our lives. Excuse me. We're preparing for an examine." I left the office before she granted permission.

...

I'd given a good amount of thought about helping the fundraising group. It really would help the people who needed financial help. So I arranged a plan to help but also benefited me. I entered the classroom where the fundraising group was meeting. 26 students, all wannabes, regardless of their ethnicity, wanting to fit in and smart enough to know with help from the fundraising group they could.

Four of the underclassmen from the football team entered behind me with my boxes. I took center stage, "This is the deal; you guys have to pass out all of these fliers for my function. And I'll pay you, the fundraising group; Eight percent of the door."

They all had been to or heard about one of mine and Shey's function, and were delighted.

"Sure! Sure!"

"That's at every high school and college in Philly."

"Sure!"

June was the first one up, and immediately divided the room into teams, assigning them to different areas in the city. She gave me a look as if I'm going to make you proud of me again.

When June and my friendship had ended, June had tried explaining she was playing them, not following them. I saw it firsthand.

Prince was sitting on a Benz's SUV, that was blocking in my vehicle. "What's what?"

"What did you say?" He was talking in code, but I didn't understand the subject.

"About?"

"I heard your name called."

I immediately lost my temper. "Man! What's the fuck is wrong with you, recommending us for therapy?"

"I wish it would've been my idea. I believe you need it."

"Get the hell out of my way. You've lost your damn mind, wanting to tell somebody our secrets. Just make sure you two make it to 'Our' function!" I hit him in the chest with a flier, then started my Range Rover."

I was the man, but I was a lady. I was disgusted with using Dora as the tester, so much that I paid three times the regular price for a tester kit.

Flacco was a little disappointed Dora wouldn't be joining us anymore.

"That's too bad, but it does leave time for us to be alone."

I ignored his advances and counted the kilos of heroin set out.

"I only want what I ordered. Keep your extra."

He only gave an impressed smile. What he didn't know was one of my clients had tried to talk me down on my price, supposedly he had found a better plug. I told him I was happy for him, and to remember all divorces are final.

CHAPTER 14

PRINCE

Day after day, the teller at the check cashing joint showed more frustration toward me, "What do you do to have so much change? How many vending machines can you rob?"

I flashed my million dollar smile at her smug look, grateful for her idea.

In my economics class I enthusiastically searched the classified ads and found several vending machines and routes for sale. They would be a way to justify my income, plus another way to bring in a legitimate income; no more being a hypocrite with Precious, and no more penitentiary chances.

Campbell had switched her study period to mine. We were spending a lot of time together at school and at least an hour in the parking lot of the hospital; studying. She was an easy person to be around, always positive with a smile, and I really enjoyed her company.

I felt good to be able to pay 25 grand on my mother's hospital bill. The clerk scanned the $500 money orders, then politely handed me my receipt with the remaining balance. My mother's bill had more than doubled. I needed more help than vending machines could provide. I put the bill away and put lotion on my mother's body. "Everyone is doing fine. Phoenix makes me so proud every day. She reminds me of you so much. She sleeps with me every night. She misses you. We all miss you mama. We'll be glad when you wake up."

I couldn't concentrate to study. I couldn't concentrate in the gym either.

Nubs didn't remain silent. He dug off in me; not babying me. "The world ain't fuckin' fair! It's what you make it or let it be! Let all that bull shit go and concentrate on what the hell you're doing! You know what? Hit the fuckin' showers! Get the fuck out of my sight with this bull shit! Something else must be more important!" He was dumbfounded when I headed out of the ring. He gave me a little clarity, the guidance I needed. It was like listening to myself, my conscience.

Nubs became speechless when he entered his office and saw me on the phone. His words wouldn't come out. All he could do was make faces. I tried to call Brooke, but her cell wasn't in service. Campbell was surprised to hear my voice, "… I need a favor?"

"Cool."

"I need to use your ride?"

She hesitated, "I'll drive you."

Nubs was really outraged when I left the gym, "You forgot to clean up!"

Campbell's smile was a relief, dependable and calming.

"Thanks for coming. I need to see a few vending machine routes, I'm thinking about buying."

"For real?"

"Yeah."

"That's cool."

The busiest locations were in the roughest areas.

"Opportunity is all around us, whether we see it or not." I liked her sarcastic humor and faces.

I was impressed by Campbell and the heavy traffic the vending machines were getting. We sat and watched each set of vending machines for 20 to 30 minutes. Unconsciously, I was rapping along with the lyrics to a song, then became blown away when Campbell rapped the second verse with much style and attitude.

"You downloaded these songs because you were picking me up?"

"No-ooo! They're my favorite."

"Let's see what else you have." I scanned every song, all were hip hop artists, and only one white artist. The more I learned about her, the more I liked her. I was in awe, staring at her.

"What's that look for?"

"Are you hungry?"

"Not really. But maybe a little."

"Pull to the drive-thru. My treat."

She was amazed by how much I ordered, then really became shocked to find out that the first part of the order was only for me, as I ordered more food for Phoenix and my brothers.

"I would hate to have to share a bathroom with you."

It was cute, but I was stuck on watching how her lips were sucking on the straw of her milkshake. "I've got one question."

Suspicion and curiosity were in her tone and facial expression, "What is it?"

"Give me the first name of a man with the last name Washington."

"Denzel. His movie starts tonight! I would love to go but I can't. I've been gone longer than I expected. I told my mother I would be right back."

I wasn't asking her out. It had been a test to learn her real mindset, her true culture. Even most people in the hood would've said George Washington but Campbell was an universal thinker.

"You can call her."

"It's a school night, I don't think so!"

It was an awkward moment when she pulled in front of my home. Neither one of us knew whether to kiss or what. We ended the night with two pounds and a smirk.

.....

Noise an influencer, physical and sematic, something that affects the understanding.

Nubs had me going over combinations when Cuda Bay entered the gym with a seamstress. Nubs was sick of the interruptions.

"This's the shit I'm talking about! This shit is interfering with your training! Where was this sponsorship some 31 fights ago? ... Everybody's gonna want a piece of you."

I paused and allowed the seamstress to quickly take my measurements while Cuda Bay preached to Nubs.

"Responsibility and interdependence of the individual, community and every establishment in the community impact upon everyone's lives, no matter what they do, their age or income. They permeate all areas. ..." Pausing to glance around the gym. "... How many members of your gym work at my company?"

"It's an even trade; a service for a fee. How many of Prince's fights have you attended?"

"If I would've been asked or invited to the fights, surely I would've acted responsibly and supported Mr. Battle."

"Give me a second, please?" Nubs gritted on me, then Cuda Bay before walking off. He was jealous of my respect for Cuda Bay. "... On one condition I'll accept your sponsorship; if I can put the emblem of the study hall on my vending machines."

"Mr. Battle, I have no problem with that."

Nubs watched Cuda Bay leave, then came over and drove me harder, coaching defensive strategies for in the ring and also in the world, swinging extremely hard, making me bob and weave. "Identify it! Look for the signs! Look for the signs! Anticipate it! Anticipate it! Don't get blindsided! The objective is to see the strong indicators and to strike first!"

...

It was a love tap, but the sting of it was mixed with anger. Precious smacked the back of my head, then stood back in silence, admiring my new Beckon's gear and my fresh fade. I was a walking bill board, and her nod of approval was supporting proof.

"You look too good to be broke. Take this." She tried to place an envelope in my hand, which I dropped instead of accepting.

The hallway at school was busy. It was the ten-minute break between classes. So, we were catching eyes.

My tone was cold and impersonal, "Don't try me like that."

It didn't faze her. She picked up the envelope of cash and played it off. "I've heard about your vending machine routs. I think it's a smart move. Four routs?"

It was the buzz on the street, most of the hood was proud of me. "Yeah. They're doing well enough to cover the mortgage. ... The routs and your promotion business, we can do this without taking penitentiary chances."

"Let me give you a truck to make it easier for you to refill your machines?"

"Are you going to quit?"

"One day. I want to pick up Phoenix and the guys, this weekend. Take them to the movies or something." Her answer was vague, so I didn't answer at first, only a you-know-better—than-to-ask-that, expression.

"When you stop."

...

One argument after the other. Creative conflicts and restrictions. Nubs was at me again because I had to stop training at 7:15 instead of eight o'clock, twice a week to restock and empty the money out of my vending machines.

"You're doing all this extra shit, when it's about boxing! Boxing is first!"

I'd bit my tongue too long, listening to his nagging. "Hell naw! My family is first! The mortgage is first! The utilities are first! Clothes are first! Groceries are first! If you're going to handle all these extras, then I won't have to miss 45 minutes, twice a week, out of my training!"

"Boxing will pay it!"

"We're living right now! Not after the Olympics!" I was doing what was best for my family, so I walked off. It wasn't open for debate.

I was washing my hair in the shower and got the feeling someone else was there. I wiped the soap from my eyes and saw Ra at the door way of the showers.

"I've got another 50 grand for you."

"I'm done with that!"

"What's the deal? You were just crying about ends to Nubs."

"That's my business. I can't help you." I was determined to do the right thing. I'd taken the chances and made the personal sacrifices, but now was the defining moment.

"Youngin' I'm getting a very bad vibe from this."

"Me too. I'm trying to take a shower while another man continues staring at me, and won't bury a dead conversation."

Ra was pissed and suspicious as he backed away from the showers. I couldn't blame him, but if I would've explained my position, he would've still felt the same way.

I left the gym being looked at as the bad guy by Ra and Nubs.

Campbell was sitting outside, studying in her SUV, which was loaded with cases of sodas and snacks. She had volunteered to help, but was hesitant about getting out near the projects, where a handful of guys were hustling.

"You're safe with me. I'm the meanest thing on earth, and the fliest! No one wants to go around with me." I showed off my foot speed and hand speed, shadow boxing, clowning.

The guys near the basketball court acknowledged me by throwing up peace signs. Campbell got out and threw several combinations at me.

"You know a little something. Huh? Show me what you're working with?"

The way she did her mouth and eyes made my blood start to boil.

"You've been all up on me. You know." Throwing a set of combos at my face.

I bobbed and weaved, got in close, then acted as if I was about to throw a hook to her face, but stopped inches from her eyes. She screamed, then hugged me. Her hands gripped my back for dear life. She was so close; her face was buried in my chest. I became instantly aroused.

"I wasn't going to hit you. You smell good."

She didn't release me, "You do to."

We were enjoying our embrace when the sirens and flashing blue lights of two police patrol units swooped on us, jumping out with their guns aimed at me.

"Let her go! And put your hands in the air!"

I couldn't believe it; it was four Black policemen acting like it was the sixties, in the deep down south.

Campbell turned around but stayed close to me while shouting at them to, "Put down your guns!"

"Why in the hell do you have your guns drawn?"

"Be quiet! ... He's my boyfriend!"

They didn't lower their weapons, "We received a call that someone was getting attacked. Ms. are you being attacked?"

"No officer. Now put away your guns!"

"Ms. move away from him."

"Put your guns away! There's no disturbance here!"

A crowd from the projects formed, "The only reason y'all fuckin' wit' them, is because she's white!"

"That's what his ass gets!" A young sister, standing in front of the crowd, mean mugging me.

Campbell went into my pocket and retrieved my wallet with my school ID and driver's license. "This is Prince Battle!"

"Is he your pimp Ms.?"

"I'm pimping your mama!"

"This is Prince Battle, soon to be representing the United States of America in the Olympics as a heavy weight boxer!"

Boxing jarred the policemen's memory. They recognized my name and face, then they lowered their guns, apologizing. "We're sorry about that man. Just doing our job. You understand. It's better safe than sorry. ... My daddy is a huge boxing and loves you. If I could get a picture with you? I've got my phone."

"It's too soon for you to be in arms' reach, let alone standing next to me for a picture."

I angrily restocked my vending machines, then rode in silence. Campbell took it as if I was mad at her. "Talk to me.?"

"I could've handled the situation."

"They would've killed you!"

"You don't know that!"

"I'm glad I can apologize for screaming at you, instead of being sorry I didn't say something, and they killed you. ... I'm sorry I screamed at you."

"Just don't let it ever ever happen again. Thank you for trying to protect your new boyfriend."

She blushed from embarrassment, "I, I, I just thought it would help."

"So, does that mean you want me as your boyfriend or not?"

She was happy we were arriving at my home. "I'll see you at school tomorrow."

CHAPTER 15

PRINCE

We forget, sleep on things we shouldn't, then when we're awakened, it startles us to realize we were unconscious.

I woke up to the loud volume of the television, blasting from the den.

"Turn that television off and take your butts to bed!"

The alarm clock read 11 PM. It seemed like the volume was raised instead of lowered. Phoenix was the only one in the den, plus she was fully dressed.

"What's your problem?"

"I promised I wouldn't tell. I'm not a snitch."

"What?" I knew it had something to do with my brothers.

"I said I wouldn't tell. But you can ask questions and find out on your own."

"Why are you dressed?"

"I'm going with you. You're taking too long. We only have to midnight, then it'll be too late."

"Pharaoh! Phihiem! I know they're not doing that midnight madness crap." They weren't in their room.

I immediately got my cell. Nubs' number went directly to voice mail. He always turned off his phone when he called it a night.

Campbell answered on the first ring, "Hey! ..."

"I'm sorry about calling so late, but I need you to come over right now. It's an emergency. You don't have time to make yourself look extra pretty. You're pretty enough."

I got dressed while fussing at Phoenix. "Remind me, you have to do 2000 sit-ups tomorrow."

"What for?"

"For not stopping them. You're the one with the most sense! You're the coach!"

Midnight madness was a block thing. I'd done it and every guy from my block had done it. It was an initiation, a bond of loyalty to our block; but someone always got caught and taken to juvenile.

Campbell had arrived. We were driving around the college campus, searching for Phihiem and Pharaoh while Phoenix quietly sat in the back seat, scrutinizing Campbell. We had dealt with white people, but it was outside of the hood, and it was a rare occasion to be riding with one, unless it was in the backseat of a police car.

I spotted Pharaoh with at least ten youngsters from our block, but I didn't see Phihiem. The crowd was looking all in the same direction at my youngest brother, walking toward a white male student who was approaching alone.

The campus was our hunting grounds, the prey was white boys and whatever they had in their pockets. It was similar to a rite of passage.

"No, no! Go there!"

I saw the brass knuckles as Phihiem placed them on his hand. Campbell whipped the SUV curbside, startling both Phihiem and the prey. I jumped out and snatched my baby brother and almost threw him inside the SUV. "You better not! Now get your butt in this car! ... Go over there."

In the eyes of the homies, what I was doing was sacrilegious, a violation of our code. It was a sensible choice to me. I ignored the comments by the guys my age from my block.

"Pee, man you're trippin'! You went through it. ... What? You're too good for the block now?"

I forced Pharaoh inside the SUV. He was mad at me but tried to take it out of Phoenix. "Lil' snitch!"

"I'm not a snitch! I didn't tell!"

"Shut up! She didn't tell me anything, I figured it out! They're your friends. We're your family! Some of them will move away, but we'll always be family! ..." I took a second to calm down, "If one of you were to get picked up, that social worker will pick up all of us and separate us. I'm not going to allow that to happen. Because we are all in each other's corner, watching each other's back! ..." Pharaoh and Phihiem were two years apart but they were inseparable like twins. "... Do you two understand? Do you two understand?"

"Yeah."

"Yeah."

"Okay then. Since you've handled that. I've got two questions."

I realized Phoenix was staring at Campbell, so I was hesitant about giving her the go ahead to ask her questions, "What are they?"

"Who is she, and what is she to you?"

I manned up, "This is Campbell. She's my girlfriend."

"Boy! Mama is going to wake up and beat your butt! I heard her tell you about gold digging fast ass girls!"

"Be quiet. Do you know what a gold digger or a fast ass girl is?" It was cute the way Phoenix shook her head. "Believe me, Campbell isn't one. Campbell, this is Phoenix, Pharaoh and Phihiem."

"What's what?"

"Do you have a younger sister?"

"Or friends that look as fine as you?"

Phoenix slapped both of them on the back of their heads.

.....

My promise, my mother's request. By breakfast I'd made my decision.

"After school, you two bring Phoenix to the gym, from now on."

All three of them stopped eating, somewhat excited, but afraid it wasn't true.

"Mom doesn't want us boxing." Pharaoh was testing the water. Our mother had said she couldn't take seeing someone punching on her babies, and since she couldn't get in the ring to help fight, no one was fighting.

"I'm the boss now." I wanted to keep an eye on them at all times. I knew the power of peer pressure.

Nubs was just as excited as my brothers, he saw the potential in both of them. "You're sure? You know how hard of a time I had with your mom about you."

"It's the only way I can keep them out of the streets."

CHAPTER 16

PRINCE

An added charge. Nubs was screaming louder than usual, and I was working extra hard, beyond the energy level I usually preformed. My tank was on E, but Nubs' motivation made me dig for more.

"Eight more days and you can lock yourself in on the Olympic team. It's all up to you! No one else! It's in your hands! Dig! Dig!"

The blots holding the body bag were being jerked with every blow I delivered. My hooks were reforming the body bag. Dust from the sand inside the body bag was trying to escape in puffs from the seams.

Two stylishly dressed white men entered the gym, which was a rare occurrence. When it did happen it was either some type of law enforcement or a bill collector. Since Nubs outright owned the building, it only meant they were the law.

Nubs stopped my session. "That's good. That's good. Hit the showers."

"Prince Battle, we would like to ask you some questions." They presented their FBI identification; Sader and Burns.

"I don't know anything and I haven't seen anything."

"Be that way. Get dressed. We'll run you in, and see how long we can hold you."

"Whoa! Hold up! What's this about?" Nubs interjected, "I'm his trainer. Who are you?"

"Special agent Sader and Burns. If you have any hope of keeping his dreams alive of going to the Olympics, I suggest you get your boxer to answer our questions."

Sader had read Nubs' concern correctly, and pushed the right button. The leverage showed in Nubs' eyes as he gritted at me.

They could apply pressure to him, but I knew if they had anything, guns would had been drawn and I would've been in cuffs. "I'll be dressed when I finish my shower."

Their expressions detailed that they both thought I would've caved in and answered whatever, "You don't even know what this is pertaining too."

"It doesn't matter, because I haven't seen anything, and I don't know about any criminal acts."

Nubs was mad, disappointed and protective. "What're you investigating? He's either in school or here all day, every day. He doesn't have time to commit a crime!"

...

The feds knew how to play a dirty game. I was frustrated from sitting in an interrogation room alone for five hours. No one had asked a question. Finally, the agents entered with smirks.

"Look kid, you don't have to throw away your career. Help us and we'll keep this on the hush. The Olympic committee doesn't have to hear about this."

"Help with what?" Since they acted as if they didn't want to tell me anything, I knew never to answer a question you don't fully understand.

"You've been identified, exchanging large sums of coins for money orders. We've got you. We have a witness willing to testify. It was clever; washing the dye money that way. But we've caught you. Give up your crew; the ones doing the actual bank robberies, and you'll never get indicted."

In my hood, snitches got found dead in ditches, and if not the snitch, his or her family.

"You have held me down here for this! I don't know anything about any bank robberies! I own 23 turnkey vending machines, that I have to restock at least twice a week. The check cashing joint is more convenient than going to the other side of town to the closest branch of the bank I do business with. Since the branch in my neighborhood closed! If I'm not under arrest I'm leaving! Excuse me!"

CHAPTER 17

CUDA BAY

There were federal agents in the showroom of my factory. Special agent Sader and Burns with several photos, superimposed, showing my symbol on the shoes and the leather bags worn and used during the bank robberies. My salesperson was entertaining their questions when I entered the room.

"Mr. Bay, we were hoping you could be of assistance." Flashing their identification for me to read.

"If I can."

"We have some high fashion bank robbers on the loose. And they're fond of your brand." Passing me the photos. Their demeanors were humble to a degree of condescension. "They're not just bank robbers, they're murders also." He was actually smiling as he studied my reaction. What normal person could smile while speaking of murder?

"How can I be of help?"

"A list of the retail stores your company does business with."

"I can manage that. If that's all, I have to excuse myself."

"Mr. Bay, do you have any samples in our size? Your prices are beyond our salaries," They wanted more time or something else, but not clothes.

"No. We only sell to retail stores."

"Do you have employee discounts?"

"For employees only. We're in a recession agents."

They stopped me again before I could leave, "Mr. Bay, can we

also get a list of your employees?"

"Once I see a court order."

They dropped their polite act, "There's other ways of getting it."

"Fine. Go about them." I calmly left the room, even though I was furiously thinking what could've led them to my company.

My secretary tried to speak but I cut him off, "Go get Ra off the floor, and tell him I need to see him in my office."

"Mr. Bay ..."

"Did I tell you to do something?"

"But ..."

"Now please!" I entered my office and had to quickly conceal my concerns because my wife was at my desk. "Will the cash flow make it to the next quarter?"

"Will you last to the next quarter?" Her attributes of intelligence, of belief; It was her intuition, but my past had given her reasoning to be weary of me.

...

A war was being raged. I knew how to fight it. They'd started a fire and I was going to blow it out with a bum. I'd made certain all my employees were at my lecture, and I'd asked all the members of the study hall to bring at least two people from the community. It was time I stepped out of the economic realm of the community and addressed the social issues the community was facing.

I'd gone out of my way to invite several local journalists. The lecture would be my stance to build a solid foundation for when the Fed's attack would come.

The amphitheater was packed to capacity. At least a thousand people had shown up. It was many people first time being in the hall. They were impressed by its design and contemporary flare.

"Recognition to our elders in the audience, that walked before us. I'm asking permission to continue to speak. ... Thank you very much." The lights dimmed and images of policemen beating Black boys, images of dead Black men, graphic images of Black-on-Black violence, were projected on to the screen. Deliberate visual shock and awe, silenced the crowd. "... We have to start deifying our own babies. That's why we have these problems in our communities. Because we have not deified ourselves. In fact, the enemy has become the deity, and in the sub consciousness of our mind we deify white folks. But we don't deify our own image. Isn't she beautiful?" A picture of the Black Madonna, looking at the Black God Child in her arms. "Some are afraid to come to our place of studying, because we talk about all this Black stuff. We tell them we're talking about the Black stuff, history, that has been since the dawn of time. History that flowed from the birth canal of the Nile Valley, that brought forth humanity onto the planet earth. Like them, I didn't know African History. Like them, I had been taught through the psychological gas chamber of the schooling system of this nation. But proof is the purist tool of truth to bring reasoning and acceptance. The heat from the light of truth burns away the clouds of lies!" The pictures projected on the screen gave credibility to my every word. "... History and artifacts corroborate the Black stuff, the history we teach. Images shape our reality. History has documented Kin Azona, the world first

Christian King long before Constantine who they try to teach is the first Christian king. They knew to make this European version of Christianity, they had to conquer one place. That place was Kemete; because Kemete had the ancient spiritual stories that the Mores were practicing, teaching the truth with the artifacts for visual evidence that went back many thousands of years. Many Mores were kidnapped from Kemete to teach many of the Romans the spiritual history.

It was Constantine who went into Kemete, into the temples and was taught the history, then tried to plaster over the ancient legacy of the history of African Christianity. He tried to make it seem as if they were the builders of the artifacts. That didn't work so they called the temples pagan, heathen, to keep people away from them, but Constantine privately kept an alter in the temples as is documented in their books; Luxor temple stands a Roman alter bearing a Latin dedication to the emperor Constantine 324 AD to 337 AD.

They took symbols like the cross that had nothing to do with crucifixion. The cross was a spiritual symbol meaning the resurrection of the spiritual body. The cross was carved in ancient sacred walls thousands of years before their versions. They came and copied symbols directly from the temples, 'With this symbol we shall conquer' ... and that's what they've been doing and is still doing."

The audience was getting more than one channel of communication.

Their minds were recording my words and the pictures on the screen.

"... Christ! Whoa, hold up Cuda Bay. Don't you talk about my white Jesus! ..." A picture, a white version of Jesus was on the screen that changed to a picture of a black Jesus that predated all pictures of Jesus.

I always added a little humor to relax the mind, to make it more receptive.

"This spiritual concept existed for thousands of years before they put their hands on it. The concept of Christ was a title placed on anyone that was known for doing good deeds, helping others. The same as the title doctor is placed on a healer. Christ had everything to do with the spirit that our ancestors called the Ca, then when the Noists got it they called it the Caress, then during the Greek and Romans' period, they called it Christ.

These subtleties seem simple, but their strength is powerful enough to make the enemy seem to be our God. It's the indoctrination of spiritual enslavement to worship their image. Even within their bible Ausar, Jesus is Black. Mary is Black, but the devil knows to see is to believe.

The white devils who have taken over our ancestral knowledge, mythology, legends and parables, beginning with the religious systems of the Egyptians! Then have the audacity to say we were uncivilized! We, as African people have always studied science and space and the universe, astronomy, the sun through the consolation. It's displayed on the temples; Amos chapter five verse eight; seek him that maketh the seven stars and Orion. The truth is carved in stone out dating the bible. ... Our ancestors saw that the sun was the physical representation of the divine force of the universe that we know by many names. One is Ra that kissed us from the dawn of time, that gave us melin. ... Palsm 84 verse 11; for the Lord God is a sun, not s-o-n, but s-u-n! They forgot to take this out, but we didn't miss it. ...

Constantinople 381 AD issued a decree to repudiate Arianism and make the Nicene creed the official creed of the Byzantine Rome government; this was the new world order of religion at that time; spiritual enslavement of the people, Ephesus 431 AD, Mary's title, the mother of God was made official and incorporated into prayers, deAfricanizing of the Goddess Aset. Webster dictionary defines Mother of God; the title of the Virgin Mary, sanctioned by the council of Ephensus 431 AD. Aset was deAfricanized at Ephensus and the European Mary was given the charactistics of Aset, making the European Mary a Virgin Goddess.

Chalacedon 451 AD declared that Christ was born of the Virgin Mary. The council also decided Christ was God and Man. ... No spiritual man came out of Europe, so they had to copy and create from our great spiritual warriors that already existed. Copying our story, our symbols. If our temples were so pagan, so heathen, why were they stealing our concepts; the virgin birth, the immaculate conception, the symbol of the cross representing peace? Because they knew they wouldn't have a story if not for our-story, the basis and foundation of today's spirituality.

Art work and artifacts are on display in Europe, date back to African art carved in stone thousands of years before European Christianity. None of this is hidden! Earlier writings prove Jesus, Ausar was burn in a cave in Ethiopia until Constantine changed it to a manger in Bethlehem. Go to Ethiopia and see Ausar, Jesus painted with his skin bronze and hair like lamb's wool. This picture predates the birth of European Christianity. One painting depicts a sword coming from Ausar's mouth. Revelation say to speak the truth to your enemy, your tongue should be like a sharp two edge sword. If I say something and no one is affected by it, I haven't said anything worthwhile.

We're going to do an imperative analytical analogy, because I want you to put this in your own mental court of law. We've heard white folks' side of the story. What we want to do now is to see our African ancestors' side of the story, then judge it for ourselves.

I'm not here for you to believe what I say. I'm not here for that. I'll let the negro preachers do that and flense you out of your money in the name of God. What I want you to do is to think because once you start thinking about what has happened, what has taken place, then you will be able to see the real spiritual light through a needle's eye. That's what I want to do because believing is seeing! ..." The projection on the screen was text, ancient text.

"Again these texts can be viewed in a museum in Romeo; The first reads Horus had two mothers: Isis the virgin, who conceived him, and Nephthys who nursed him. He was brought forth singularly as one of five brothers. The bible reads; Jesus had two mothers, Mary the virgin, who conceived him and Mary the wife of Ceophus who brought forth as one of her children. He was brought forth singularly as one of five brethren. The first reads: Hoarus was with his mother, the virgin until twelve years old, when he was transformed into the beloved son of God as the only begotten of the father on earth. The bible reads: Jesus remained with his mother, the virgin until twelve years, when he left her to be about his father's business. The first reads: From twelve to thirty years of age there is no record in the life of Hoarus. The bible reads: From twelve to thirty years of age there is no record in the life of Jesus. The first reads: Hoarus at thirty years of age became adult in his baptism by Anup. The bible reads: Jesus at thirty years of age made a man in his baptism by John the Baptist. The first reads: Hoarus in his baptism made transformation into the beloved son and only begotten of the father; the holy spirit, represented by a bird. The bible reads: Jesus in his baptism is hailed from Heaven as the beloved son and the only begotten of the father, the holy spirit, that is represented by a dove.

Our story, their story, see how easily they converted Isis and Hoarus, Aset and Ausar to Mary and Jesus. ..."

The majority had the glow and happiness of containing something new, I'd planted the seed for the fight to come. I made my way to my office, Ra, Melik and the others were there, waiting. It was the only times we could be seen together. I had scheduled the meeting to see if it was a coincident, luck or stupidity that led the feds to our door front.

"Can anyone think of a reason?" Ra's face showed the signs of stress, "What is it?"

"I didn't burn the dye money. But before you start, I don't think it has anything to do with the feds showing up."

"What did you do with the money! What did you do with the dye money!"

"We sold it for a dime on the dollar. ... "To Prince. The kid from my session group. His family is in need, with his mother ..."

"I know his story." I liked Prince. I'd watched him develop into a man, a strong soldier.

"The kid is cut like us."

"We're going to let this play out, but at the first sign that he's not thorough, you have to correct your error."

...

Just as I had thought, my lecture made the next day's newspaper. The article wasn't as controversial as I wanted, but it was the top headline on page 3A; the number of people in attendance, the economic power in the community, then asking could teaching the truth, be the same as teaching hate.

The light on my phone flashed. "Yes."

"There's a problem in the parking lot."

The AM shift was getting off and the PM shift was arriving, Special agent Sader and Burns along with my ex-probation officer, were harassing my employees to answer questions. I was furious that they were on my property, but delighted to find out they didn't have anything other than hunches or they wouldn't have been trying so hard to find something, anything on the robberies.

"If you've got questions for any of my employees, call them to your office or meet them at their homes. I will not allow you to hinder the production of my company! Get off my property!"

"Or what?" They thought they had the power of authority, but authority is given, meaning it can be given as well as taken away. On the other hand, the love and respect my employees had for me; I had earned. It showed when over 115 men and women started to gather, readying for battle.

"I'm going to say this one more time; Get off my property!"

"You have a nice day Mr. Bay. I promise you'll be seeing more of us." All three backed off the premises of my parking lot.

CHAPTER 18

PRINCE

The statement of benefits, the reason why, supporting, justifying the proposition; the main purpose of which is to render the message as convincing as possible.

Pharaoh and Phihiem's high enthusiastic level of conditioning, training drew Nubs' Attention. He made his way over, watching and listening to the way Phoenix was encouraging while driving the boys.

"You are the best! So train like the best! Show me you're the best! Prove it!"

Phoenix's method was the same as our mother, never tearing down, but always building up.

It was interestingly different to Nubs, but he acknowledged the effectiveness. "Lil' coach tell them to do it more like this." Demonstrating for my brothers to see. Nubs' basic formula for training the fundamentals; You hear, you forget; you see, you remember; you do it, you understand. "Shift your weight with your punches, to give your punch more power. Keep your elbows high. Always protect yourself, even when you throw a punch."

"When are we going to get to spar?"

"Get into the ring!"

"I don't want to fight my brother!"

"I don't have anyone your age here."

"He's my size. What about him?" Pharaoh was at the top end of a light weight.

"Yo, Que? Pharaoh is calling you out!"

"I ain't trying to go to war with Pee for punishing his fam."

Phoenix answered the indirect insult. "Just say you're scared!"

I entered the gym to see Que and Pharaoh exchanging blows, toe to toe, blow for blow in the center of the ring. Neither backing down until Phoenix shouted, "L. H! ..."

At first I was tempted to jump into the ring and punish Que, but I stopped in amazement, seeing Pharaoh deliver a liver, head to liver combination, that made Que try to grab him.

Phoenix was beating on the mat, screaming, "S-B-U! S-U-B!"

Pharaoh followed her coded instructions; sliding, bobbing, then came up with an upper cut that caught Que square on the button, sending him to the ropes. Nubs quickly grabbed Pharaoh, stopping him from finishing Que. We were so proud of Pharaoh, that we all ran into the ring to celebrate.

.....

There are three fundamental elements in communication; sender, message, receiver.

The sender is active, while the receiver is passive.

It was the day before the fight. All of us except Precious, were at the hospital visiting our mother. I was anxious at being one step closer to making the Olympic team and winning a gold medal. I could feel my mother's hand gripping mine tighter as I spoke, "It feels like it's my first fight all over again. I'm not scared. I just want to hear the bell and be able to get it over with. I know I have to be patient. I'm not going to rush into anything. I just wish you ..."

My mother's eyes opened. She didn't speak but her eyes darted to whoever moved.

"Mama! Mama!

"Mom, say something."

We all were excited, but I tried to keep the others calm.

"Pharaoh go get the nurse."

"I've got it." Phoenix pressed the button for the nurse.

Nurse Pottier entered the room and became just as excited.

"Thank you Jesus! Thank you!" She quickly left, then returned with the doctor. He checked my mother's vitals and was puzzled.

"We're not sure what this means. This could be temporary. I'll schedule her for more tests."

HIs uncertainty didn't affect or interfere with the message of hopefulness we were feeling.

My mother's grip, the passion in her eyes, the income from the vending machines, the fact that once the bell would ring, I would be in control of my life: all of it had me hyped.

.....

The up-tempo rap was the only thing keeping me calm while Nubs taped my hands. He started to give me a motivational speech but didn't once looking into my eyes. "You know what you have to do."

There's an art and a science to boxing. I put on a beautiful brutal, bedazzlement of punishment. The ref had to stop the fight in the third round.

My ears toned in on Precious screaming. I spotted her joyful smile of feeling the accomplishment of reaching our goal. Jumping, celebrating our victory.

Campbell was just as loud and excited, looking up at me from ring side.

The Hammer and his father were trying to leave ring side when the reporters blocked the Hammer's path.

"Who will you fight now, since the champ has been banned from boxing?"

"Whoever gets into the ring." Then he pushed his way through the crowd.

.....

There were three floors to the club, each with its own DJ. Each floor packed to capacity. Half-naked females splashed around in giant martini glasses, G-string wearing muscle men were in hanging cages. A live rap group was being showcased on the middle floor. The atmosphere of the party was astonishing. The crown to cap off how I was feeling: On top of the world with Campbell close to me. She had really dolled up; her clothes were fly and more skin revealing. The way her body swayed to the beat, I could tell she was also feeling the energy.

We were grooving on the dance floor when she turned toward me and passionately kissed me in front of everyone, while still dancing.

"Are you ready to go?"

"Are you sure you're ready to do this?"

We'd talked about sex, but since she was a virgin, I hadn't pressed the issue.

I just hinted she'd still be a virgin if she just did oral sex.

"Let me use the restroom, then we can leave."

I saw Precious looking over her accomplishment. She had perfectly organized everything.

"We're out. Nice, nice jam! Great job! Thank you for promoting me."

"Use a condom. Bye boy." She didn't like being seen as soft, so she hugged me, then pushed me away.

Before I made it to the hallway of the restrooms, Brooke stopped me. "Congratulations. You did it."

"Yeah. Whoa, you look nice. Thanks for coming out." I surprised her with a hug, finalizing our conversation. I felt her sigh in my arms, then I released her to go to Campbell's smiling face who was waiting at the entrance of the club.

.....

I did everything to try to make Campbell feel comfortable; holding her hand while she drove, kissing her finger tips. I really didn't want her to change her mind. She'd gotten a luxurious hotel suite. She answered my impressed look. "I don't think I would be able to go through with this at your house with your brothers and Phoenix there."

She'd burned a special CD of slow hip hop jams just for the occasion, to help the mood.

I could see my massiveness was scaring her as I started to undress, so I dimmed the lights.

Her eyes kept darting toward my member, "You do remember I've never done this."

"For real?"

She smiled, then playfully pushed me. I kissed her deeply, then tried to be as sensuous and gentle as possible as I kissed down to her breasts, giving both equal attention before going down on her until she squealed at orgasm.

I then admired her beauty, her curves. I kissed her again, distracting her. I felt the intensity of her body stiffening as I entered her. Our bodies melted into one to the rhythm of the music. She sighed and moaned, enduring the pleasurable pain, which became a high pitch squeal, then a tremble flowed through her body. She held me so tightly it seemed for dear life. I could see she was crying, so I kissed her salty tears.

CHAPTER 19

PRECIOUS

An important part of the effort. At one o'clock the crowd to enter the club was still two city blocks long. I'd upgraded Chub and West's attire. West stood as the bouncer at the door while I and Chub chilled in the VIP section; Chub stood guard, keeping the so-called ballas from bothering me. I was sick of guys asking to buy me a drink, when I had bought the entire club for the night.

Four members of the fundraiser club tried to chill with me. I'm 100 percent me, and I respect people for what they are. So since I knew the only reason those girls wanted to be around me, was to look important; which was fake. So I signaled Chub to block their way. They left pissed and embarrassed, but June stopped, then returned to the VIP section. She semi shouted around Chub. "I'm sorry about your mother and Shey, but you're not alone in this world. It's people that still care about you."

June's eyes looked sincere, before she left.

June's boyfriend was a petty hustler that wanted to be a big-timer. He had found a niche for himself and was determined to come up. He sold ecstasy in the form of candy suckers, in the local clubs.

He was watching June from the bar as she returned from the VIP section.

"That's Shey's girl, huh? ... She's taken over his promotional business. You think she might be moving work on the side? ... You and her?"

June was bisexual. She and I had experimented once, but it didn't seem right. "Once upon a time."

"Yeah. Good. Go comfort your friend. Don't fall in love. Find out what you can. Here." He passed June a knot of cash and some suckers.

June gave the girls from the group the suckers. "I'll catch up with you all later." She then pre-tipped the waitress to follow her with a bottle of champagne to the VIP section. I nodded to Chub that it was okay for June to sit.

"You look like you need somebody to talk to. I'll just listen and sip." June smiled deviously before she proudly paid the waitress.

It was like old times, but instead of cool aid, we talked and drank Mascato until the club was empty, except for the owner and the wait staff who were cleaning up.

The owner came to the table with two checks, smiling at me, then checking out June, while I verified the door count with West.

I caught June cutting her eyes to the amounts of the checks.

"Should we lock in the dates we were discussing?"

"Excuse me?" I was buzzed, but he wasn't my type. He was too old.

"The date for your next function."

"I'm trippin. I thought you were popping at me."

"Should I be?"

June rudely answered, "No!"

It kind of threw me, but she'd made me feel better, so I only smirked at her.

June and I both needed Chub's help getting into the back seat of the Land Rover.

The vibrating bass and the touch of June's hand on my tight had a tingling sensation coursing through my body. I felt the heat building. Her eye contact, a confident gaze, knowing what she was doing. I could hear my heart beat. The rush of blood had enlarged both of our nipples. I grabbed her hand stopping her, not because it didn't feel right. It was because it felt too right, and if I didn't stop her then, I wouldn't had wanted her to stop.

"Boss lady, where're we headed?"

"Are you going home?" June only shook her head. "Take us in."

.....

My bed was too big for one person. June's kisses were soft and gentle, so light, so delicate of a touch. Passionate, affectionate, the warmth, the caring, the feeling of being understood. Gender didn't matter. It wasn't sex. It was love making; spiritual.

.....

It felt good waking up next to somebody, until seeing the mismatched underwear and knock-offs; the imitation gear on the floor next to my bed. I immediately decided to upgrade Junes' wardrobe.

"There's new underwear in the drawer. I'm sure something in my closet will fit you. It's a new tooth brush in the medicine cabinet."

After a shower and breakfast, we shopped until we dropped. It was so arousing picking out clothes, then watching June modeling for me.

I bought as much or more for my brothers and Phoenix than I did for June.

Prince had changed the locks to the house. It pushed my button, and I ordered Chub to kick the door off the hinges.

.....

I wasn't lonely anymore. I was openly with June. We would hold hands in the hallways at school, kiss in public, everything about us was intimate. It quickly spread around the school, but I didn't care until Prince snatched me up at my locker. The look in his eyes made me feel nasty. His disappointment belittled me.

"What's wrong with you! Have you gone crazy? I mean, you broke into the house! You're running around here kissing and carrying on with her like it's the thing to do!"

Tears formed instantly, but I wasn't going to allow them to drop.

"You don't understand!"

"Make me understand. Help me, so I can help you."

"I can't make you understand. It's not about sex. Maybe if we all got back together as a family." I wanted the support of my family. I did want his help.

"When you stop all this nonsense, but not until then. I'm not allowing you to bring any of this shit around us." He looked at me as if I was a disgrace.

.....

The various and different objectives to be achieved. June had borrowed a car to supposedly go to her mother's place to pick up something. I didn't mind; I didn't have to make up an excuse to leave her at the house while I handled my business.

Instead, June went to her boyfriend's apartment. He was pouring ecstasy suckers into the molders, "Damn, I thought you had jumped ship."

"I need some money."

"I should be asking you! Look at you. All brand new. You're doing the damn thing."

"I need some money. I want to get her something special."

"Is she in the game or not?"

"She's into something, but I don't know what. I'm working my end, just give me a little time. I need the money."

Semi mad he took out a knot.

"I need three, but two might do it."

"Here." June accepted the money and turned to leave but her boyfriend grabbed her wrist. "Damn, don't you want some dick? Because I need a shot of pussy bad as a muthafucka!"

"I don't have time. I told her I was running by my mom's."

"Okay, that's a good excuse."

"I don't have my soap or my lotion or my perfume that I use. Not this time."

"Shit, use your old shit."

"I can't! She'll be able to tell. She's a woman. We notice shit like that."

"You better give me some head or something and brush your teeth!"

.....

My confusion had me irritated. Everything was conflicted. I was scanning the sport section of the newspaper. There was a small, five sentence paragraph about Prince, but four pages about the dumb ass heavy weight champ testing positive for steroids for the third time, negating any appeal of the boxing commissioner's decision of banning him from boxing.

June entered the room, noticed my tension, then tried to massage my neck and shoulders. "You're still having headaches?"

I turned so that her hands came off of me. I didn't feel like being touched.

"You should go to the hospital and get it checked. It could be something that can become serious."

"A fuckin' bullet went through my head! Is that, not serious? Please stop acting so dumb! You are brilliant. Be proud of it!" Nothing set me off more than someone pretending to be passive or weak, seeking to gain leverage.

"Here! I hope this make you feel better! Pissed at me for no damn reason. I haven't done shit to you; but love you." She couldn't have played the situation better, if she had planned it. She gave me a new lap top.

I'd left mine in Shey's car and hadn't had time to buy another. The gesture itself touched me.

"Thank you. I'm sorry. I'm just pissed about the little coverage Prince is getting."

"Write your own blog. Make it grand. Tell the real story of your brother. Write your picture, you want the world to see. ... Start a sports blog from a female's perspective. You can do it. You've always been a great writer. You always said you were going to be an author and a journalist. Why wait until you go to college? Start now!"

"You remember that?"

"Yes. I remember everything you told me. Write your blog. I'm going to take a quick shower."

My article was conflicting. A sad story, but a hero was born. My objective was to attract attention and interest to my brother. I linked my blog to sport sites, newspaper editorials and tragedy sites. My five-page article received national attention and brought in support and sympathy for Prince and for our mother. The Instagram and Facebook pages I created for Prince were instantly threading sensation.

CHAPTER 20

PRINCE

A frightening capacity to follow orders.

Pharaoh and Phihiem were working out with me; jumping rope, hitting the speed bag, doing foot work drills to Nubs' commands. It was strange for Phoenix to be to herself, with her head in her book, while at the gym.

"Lil' Coach, don't you supposed to be coaching or doing exercises yourself?"

She only gave me a sad look and I immediately smacked the back of my brothers' heads, "What did you all say to her?"

"Nothing! She's been like that since we picked her up from school."

She was my heart. I couldn't stand to see her so down.

Nubs shot me an evil look as I stopped in the middle of an exercise and went to my sister's side. I couldn't let her think that she was alone, regardless what she was feeling."

"What's what?" Only a head shake, "Man, what's what?" Honest communication was what we thrived on, never feeling afraid to express ourselves. Then I saw a tear fall from Phoenix's eyes, "Tell me what's wrong now!"

"I can't,"

"Girl, if you ..." I had to calm myself. "We're family. You can tell me."

"I can't."

"Did your brothers say something to you?"

"No. It's nothing to do with them."

"We are family. You can tell me."

"If I tell you, we won't be a family anymore. They'll split us up."

More tears. She was becoming emotional which scared me because I knew it was serious. Our mother had a thing about tears, "... crying doesn't solve a damn thing, so why are you crying?" We all hated crying. "Does this have something to do with Precious?"

"No. I can't tell her either."

"If it's something that you can't handle, telling me is not snitching. Can you handle whatever this is?"

"I'm not tough enough."

I absorbed her pain. I wanted to cry too, "Okay, since you're not tough enough, I'm sure you're smart enough to tell me – since I'm tough enough. Then we both can think of a way to handle it without tearing our family apart. Okay?"

"He touched me. Here, here, and here and on my butt."

"Who!"

"Mr. Branchard."

"Your teacher?"

"Yes. I punched him a lot, but he only laughed and kept touching me. And told me if I tell anyone, that we would be separated and put into different foster homes." She cried in my arms.

I wanted to find out where Mr. Branchard lived and kill him.

"I'm going to handle it in the morning. Now you have to be my Lil' coach. Plus, your brothers need you, because you're better than Nubs."

.....

Each passing hour of the night was a thinking period where my rage and reasoning battled.

Phoenix had told Pharaoh and Phihiem, so we all were waiting outside the principal's office of Phoenix's elementary school. We were individuals but we gathered strength from our family core, of knowing we were in it together.

My reasoning was controlling my rage. The eight o'clock bell rang.

"Pharaoh, you and Phihiem go ahead to class. I can handle it."

8:27, the principle's secretary came out. "He won't be in until nine o'clock."

I put my feelings into action. I took Phoenix's hand and led her directly to her fourth-grade class. I had tried to give the school system the chance to handle it.

The timid expression of fear was on the face of the teacher when Phoenix and I entered the class room.

"Excuse me? I'm Prince Battle, Phoenix's older brother. Can I discuss something with you in the hallway?"

The teacher quickly picked up his walkie talkie and immediately started screaming, "Security! Security! Please report to room 205!"

I released Phoenix's hand and landed an overhanded left on the temple of the man, that knocked him into the black board.

My combination of head shots split his face and sent blood gushing from the cuts over the teacher's eyes, from his nose and his mouth. He fell to the floor unconscious, and I tried to stomp the remaining life out of him.

The children in the room became fearful that I had killed their teacher. The security guards arrived, but then recognized me and decided to wait on back up before rushing me, tackling me.

I could hear Phoenix screaming, "He has been touching us! Stop it! Stop it! He has been touching us! He waits until we go to get our sweaters, then touches us like he's helping to put it on! Tell them! Tell them!" Screaming at the other students, then screaming in fright once seeing me being tazed.

.....

Influencing the views; Cameras were flashing and news teams were everywhere as I was led in hand cuffs inside the police precinct by six police men.

I noticed special agent Sader, talking with a younger Black guy who was dressed in fly street clothes. I could see the Black guy's badge dangling from a necklace around his neck.

Sader immediately approached me, "Well, well, what do we have here?"

One of the officers answered, "An assault on a school teacher."

The Black agent had followed Sader over. "Damn, he's still in school!"

Principle Ellary entered the precinct, then hurried over as the officers were placing me in a holding cell. "The school isn't pressing charges. You can release him."

"Wait. Sir, he attacked a school teacher!"

Ellary eyed Sader, then in a defensive tone, "He attacked a known pedophile, that's been caught several times, but resigned to avoid prosecution, and the school district allowed it, to avoid embarrassment."

"Sir, can you wait a week to drop the charges? This kid is not a rose. He's under investigation for some serious crimes."

"Detective."

"No. I'm a special government agent."

"I apologize, Special agent. I've been a teacher or a principle for 22 years, and I've seen my share of children boxed in, criminals in the makings. Prince Battle is exceptional, not only at boxing but as a person. As big as he is, he has never been the bully, but the protector. He's going to be much greater than a rose. ... A few months ago his mother was put into a coma. He's caring for his brothers and sisters. This city loves him, and one day the world will too."

"He has everyone fooled."

"My job as an educator is to help students reach their full potential. I don't know what special agents do, but I suspect you do. I'm not going to interfere with your investigation, but I'm dropping the charges as of now. Will you please release Prince Battle?"

....

Communicating information, cannot be taken for granted; the potential channel can distort to alter the message to suit their own views or ambitions, to influence attitudes and behaviors, making it genuinely difficult to be objective.

Nubs was in his office, watching the news and answering and hanging up his cellphone. The frustration made him throw the cellphone against the wall. Then he realized I was standing in the doorway of his office.

"If I had some muthafuckin' hair, I would be pulling it out about now! What the hell is going on? Why are you self-destructing? … You assaulted one of your teachers?"

"If you believe that, you're not thinking straight!"

"The shit is all over the news! What am I supposed to believe?"

"Me! Believe me damn it! You know me! Ask me what happened!"

"Did you do it?"

"Yeah, but …"

"But hell! If you don't want to go to the Olympics, just tell me. Fuck! Prince? This is our dream!"

"Man, a sick perverted muthafucka has been molesting Phoenix, and over half of her classmates! What was I to do! I had no choice! ... What did the Olympic committee say anyway?"

We both were frustrated and stressed.

"They haven't made their decision yet. Get dressed. Workout time! Ain't a damn thing changed."

Half way through the session Precious and my brothers and Phoenix arrived. Nubs just walked away once I stopped and went to Phoenix.

"Are you all right?"

"Yeah. What did the tazer feel like?"

Once I growled at Phoenix, she hugged me.

Precious was furious, "Excuse me. When you learned about this why didn't you call me? I am a part of this family!" I didn't say a word. My expression said it all. Precious became timid. "You guys go ahead and start your workout."

"No, they need to hear this; just in case they're not sure. You have been banned from this family until you get your shit together. I don't want you around us until then."

Campbell was standing in the background, then stepped forward, involving herself into the conversation. "Prince, don't do that! She's your sister. What if something happens to you in the ring?"

"This is my family! My responsibility! You don't have a say in how I run it!"

Precious stopped Campbell from speaking, "Don't waste your breath. I'm out of here. ... I'm still a part of this family! And you know it!"

My sparring partners both only lasted one around. Nubs was so impressed he ended the session early.

We all rode in silence until Campbell broke the hush, "I see how big you're on family. I was only trying to keep the situation calm. She is who she is, you might have to accept that. ... I want to introduce you to my dad. Maybe he can help. He knows a lot of influential people"

I didn't answer. I wasn't in the mood for talking. Just a kiss.

"Thanks for the ride. We're see you later."

The drama continued the next morning; the social worker that had come to the hospital was at my school talking to my teachers. I waited until she was about to walk away, then approached her. "Are you asking questions pertaining to me?"

"I'm just doing my job."

"My mother is getting better! Why are you harassing me?"

"I'm just doing my job. Taking on adult responsibilities can be stressful and put people under a lot of pressure. Someone prone to violence might become unstable to care for other children. Are you under pressure?"

It was a trick question. She didn't understand how thoroughly entrenched self-defense is in Blacks, so I walked away from her.

Campbell was at our locker.

"Yes, I need you to introduce me to your dad."

"How about next Saturday and Sunday?"

"Fine with me."

She was excited, but I was hoping he could really help.

CHAPTER 21

PRINCE

To take in and make part of an existent whole.

Since we were going to meet Campbell's father, I thought it was only fair she met our mother when we stopped by the hospital.

"Why don't you come up with us?"

"Yeah, it might make mom get up and kick his butt. But once she gets to know you, I'm sure she'll like you." Phoenix took a hold of Campbell's uncertain hand.

Once in the hospital room Campbell's expression showed she'd absorbed our pain. I placed Campbell's hand inside my mother's, then Campbell learned where we got our strength.

"Mom, this's Campbell, my new girlfriend."

"Nice to meet you Mrs. Battle. I've heard such nice things about you. I hope, I pray we get to know one another." Campbell tried to fight back her tears but couldn't.

We updated our mother on the details in our lives, then gave kisses and said our good-byes.

Campbell excitedly talked about how her father and I would hit it off, because we were so much alike.

Phoenix interrupted Campbell, being too mature for her age. "Except Prince is Black."

We were all silenced with amazement by the size of the estate, the massive hotel size home.

"This is where you grew up?"

"Yes."

I could tell her parents had money by the vehicle she drove, but I never imagined they could afford what I was seeing.

"Does it have a pool like a hotel?"

"Yes. Two, and they're both heated. Let me show you to your rooms, and we can take a swim before dinner."

Phoenix and my brothers became really excited.

No one was home except the maid. The inside of the building was luxurious, and easily topped every home I'd seen on Cribs, the television show.

Campbell played hostess, showing my brothers and Phoenix to their rooms first. My room was on the far end of the hallway.

"Where's your room?"

"On the other end, next to my dad's." Then teased me with a kiss before leaving. I dove across the huge bed like a big kid.

I was only in my gym shorts when the door eased open. It was Campbell with a devious smirk. While locking the door behind her, Campbell purposefully dropped the wrap scarf from around her waist, revealing the bottom half of a two-piece swim suit. The curves of her body gave me an instant hard-on. Ass, hips and thighs. Thickness with a small waist and a flat defined stomach, plus the perfect set of tits.

As soon as I'd tossed her on the bed there were knocks at the door.

"Prince tell'em; with one big fight when you turn pro, you'll be able to buy us a house like this!" It was Phoenix and my brothers.

"They might go away if I don't answer."

More knocking came. "Prince, unlock this door! We saw you come down here Campbell! We know you two are in there!"

Once Campbell had fixed her scarf around her hips, I opened the door. "Two homes like this, but after I win the gold in the Olympics."

Pharaoh gave me a look like he thought I was crazy. "Why wait to turn pro!"

Phoenix answered him like it was a stupid question. "Because a gold metal will make him more marketable."

"How do you know?"

"I'm the brains. I'm the Lil' Coach! So, listen to me!"

Pharaoh blew Phoenix off and directed his question at me. "Don't we need the money now?"

Phihiem was staring at Campbell's ass and legs. "Where are your sisters!"

"I only have a big brother."

I was listening to all of them, but I felt Pharaoh's passion in his question.

Before I could add anything Phoenix's answer. "We will make more money after he wins the gold in the Olympics!"

I was shocked to see the Hammer and Mr. Bosco at the bottom of the stairs.

"So you're the one who has my daughter dressing like a lady instead of a boy?"

I stayed composed, even though I felt played, "Mr. Bosco, with no disrespect meant, if Campbell would've told me you were her father, I would've never come here, or gotten involved with her. You guys go get dressed and pack your bags. We're leaving."

"You're over reacting. You're tripping." Campbell sounded so sincere.

"The Olympic committee is still undecided about me. I don't need any more shady questions about my character. Did I say to go get dressed? Go!"

"Son, I can help."

"I imagine you could, but at what price? Everyone you've called yourself helping, ends up with the short end of the stick."

The Hammer stepped toward me, "Don't be disrespectful to my father!"

"It's a difference between disrespect and speaking honestly to a man. Mr. Bosco, no thank you for your offer to help."

Campbell's eyes were pleading her case, "I'll take you home?"

"No thank you."

She followed me to the room. "Let me explain."

"Stop it. All I want to do is call an uber, then we're getting the hell away from you."

I closed the door in her face.

Campbell stood outside with us, trying to explain while we waited. I toned her out.

The uber took us to the Greyhound bus station, which we took back to Philly.

.....

Running to free myself, seeing the sun coming, pushing myself to sprint the step of the art museum. The rap, the cool freshness from the season changing, all zoned out my thoughts. The arrival of people going to their jobs made me realize the time, Phoenix had breakfast ready when I got home.

I arrived late for my first period. I ignored Campbell, even at the bus stop. "How are you going to restock your machines? Let me help, please?"

At the hospital I stretched and messaged my mother, reminiscing about her racing after me, down the block, trying to whup my butt. Then her hugging me, encouraging me, proud of me after seeing my report card. I put my report card back into my pocket. "We need you mom. I need you. I'm not sure I can do this by myself. Please come back to us?"

I was wondering if I'd bitten off more than I could chew. My sorrow turned to laughter as I realized I was hungry.

I surprised Nubs when I entered the gym earlier than normal, "I need to use your van."

"Don't you supposed to be at the hospital?"

"I need to use your van to restock my machines and pick up my change. If I do it now, it won't interfere with my training."

He tossed the keys, "Where's that fine ass white girl? Your Lil' shit ain't working? That's why you keep losing your women?"

"Seems to me, they're the one losing out. I'm the prize catch, that got away."

"The committee people said they'll make their decision the first week of November. So, don't kill anybody with my shit!"

.....

Interpret and apply. I was in class, taking a test when my name was announced over the intercom to report to the principal's office.

"You can finish your test when you return."

"I'm finished."

My locker was on the way to the office. The police were searching it. "Why the hell are you in my locker!"

The assistant principle was with the police, "I'll handle this. Principle Coffee is waiting on you."

Special agent Sader was in the office laughing and flirting with the principle. "I appreciate this."

"It's nothing. But I don't think Prince would involve himself with bank robbers. He's an excellent student and a good person."

The school secretary saw me eavesdropping and buzzed the principle. "Prince Battle is here. ... Go ahead."

The principle was pleased to see me. "Prince, special agent Sader needs you to accompany him to the precinct."

"Principle Coffee, I've spoken with this agent before. If he's not arresting me, I have no farther need to discuss anything with him."

Her demeanor became more authoritative. "I understand, but if you have any information that could be helpful. It is your civic duty to help. There's a code of conduct that can call for your expulsion. I recently had a conversation with the Olympic committee and told them you are a fine candidate to represent our great nation in front of the world. I can always call them back and tell them I made a mistake, if you refuse to go to the precinct and answer special agent Sader's questions, that might stop some criminals."

The bell rang as we were leaving the office, so most of the school saw me getting into the unmarked Charger.

Sader's tone was filled with envy and hatred. "Everyone vouches for you. They love you. You are truly the peoples champ. But I know somehow you're mixed up with this."

At the precinct, all the holding cells were filled with the ex-cons that worked for Beckon's factory. Sader paraded me by the cells on the way to an interrogating room. Inside was a middle age white man with tight skin that made him look as if he was frowning even when he wasn't.

"I'm district attorney Jurroda. I know who you are, what you're going through, and I know you're involved. I'm only going to ask you one question, and this is your only time to free yourself. If you don't use it, when I give the bank robbers a hundred years, you will receive it too. Who gave you the dye money?"

"Like I've told special agent Sader; no one has given me any dye money! I've answered your question. Can I go?"

"Special agent Sader, please take Mr. Battle back to school?"

"I'll catch the bus!"

CHAPTER 22

CUDA BAY

Rules are not necessarily laws, but a law is a rule of civil conduct, that's enacted and enforced.

I and at least one hundred and ten of my employees had been called to the precinct for questioning. We all had been waiting for hours in holding cells until the last one had answered Sader and the DA's questions.

"Where were you on the dates of June 1st, and 19th, July 21st, July 28th, August 4th and 5th, September 27th and 29th, during the time of 4:30 PM until 5:00 PM?"

"At work, except on Fridays and Saturdays, or at the study hall. I work 80-hour weeks."

"You've done time before for bank robberies?"

"I've paid for my short comings. I now run a legitimate business."

"Maybe the recession made you backside? Money got low. A quick lick to stay afloat. You know how the story goes. Give up your crew before they give you up. What you'll get compared to what they get, will be a light slap on the wrist or you can do the hundred years. We're going to work with whoever works with us."

"I have a business to run. Are we done?"

They had a theory, but nothing to prove it. They kept us in the holding cells for a few more hours. I watched the frustration, the bickering. My employees were mad for being detained for no apparent reason.

·····

By the time I arrived home my entire house was dark. CB2 was asleep and only rolled over when I kissed his cheek and put the covers over him; a treasure I was willing to do anything for.

When I entered my bedroom, my wife was sitting up in bed, in the dark, holding her knees against her chest.

"I promise you, if you let them take you to prison again I will divorce you, and you will never be in CB2's life again. Whatever you're doing or have done! Stop now. Stop now. We can sell the business."

I could tell by the way she was breathing that she was crying. She pushed me away when I tried to comfort her.

"Don't touch me! Listen to me! Stop it! Please? I don't want to be without you."

There had been bids to buy my clothing line. The money would've had my family set for generations, but the bids didn't include keeping the factory in Philly. The manufacturing of the clothes would've been moved to Korea. My dream wasn't about money, it was about helping my community by employing people, providing medical insurance.

My strategy was simple, keep building the base. I had members and employees going door to door with fliers announcing the factory was hiring for a graveyard shift; with Christmas approaching, the factory had gotten back logged and the shift was seasonal.

.....

Most of the community was in the parking lot along with every employee of my factory. My security was setup the same as if I was lecturing in the hall.

"Before I allow anyone into the factory, I want to address the rumors that are circulating in the community and in my factory. ..."

As I was speaking a bank lick was going smoothly wrong. The job was perfectly executed but as the designer suit robbers were existing the bank, a police patrol unit was in the drive-thru and began to shoot at them, hitting one of the bank robbers in the back of the neck. The bullet exited the front of his throat and burst a car window. A shoot out ensued. The robbers took cover behind cars in the parking lot, but the police men had only their car for cover. The bullets from the automatic weapons of the remaining robbers riddled the patrol unit; tires exploded, glass burst, the engine smoked and leaked, then one of the robbers walked up to the patrol unit and sprayed the already dead officers at point blank range. The others checked the downed robber, who was bleeding to death, while trying to hold his neck to stop the blood from pouring out.

Eye contact. A wordless agreement, then a quick mercy kill from the robber returning from the police unit.

...

"... Somebody knows something about us that they don't want us to know about ourselves. We're causing our own suffering by deifying white folks. Worshipping a white woman, little white babies, instead of our own babies and women. We can't envision our dreams because we're too busy dreaming about what we see on television. To reach our dreams we must wake up or we will only be dreamers. This is why we're catching so much hell in our community with gang banging because we're not deifying our babies and women and men as a God in the universe. If we believe we are in the image of God, when we see ourselves we must be able to see God. If we deify our babies as a God, they will grow up as a divine spirit and will not hurt the community. The white devils know this, and they fear the black seed.

Because we are growing out of the ideas inculcated since slavery; Each succeeding generation of our children will be progressively assertive of its manhood. I repeat, all that our people lack, is training and opportunity. We don't have to tickle the color-vanity of the whites. Their thoughts, their diabolical actions to take the victimization off the people, and to make themselves look like the victims and the people as if we are the perpetrators, the heathen. They put it off on us, the people; as if we are at fault, not the failed system. The devils keep us from seeing who is really the cause. Then they throw the new game out at us; reverse racism. Yes! I'm a reverse racist! Because I've been a victim of racism! And I'm responding to racism. If you have a coin and you flip it over it's still a coin. It's the same with racism. ..."

Ra and Malik made eye contact with me once back in position.

"...The truth has to be in relationship with the arena it is in."

.....

A manhunt was being announced over every media in my home. I sat in my front room, with my front door opened, waiting, knowing the swat unit would eventually storm my home.

My wife had taken CB2, vowing to live up to her promise.

I couldn't explain my plan to her. I didn't want her directly involved.

At 4 AM the law ransacked my home and arrested me.

The PPD was heated over the death of two of their finest. The judge had rubber stamped the search warrant and the DA had played on the emotions of the moment to manipulate a grand jury to get indictments for me, Ra, Malik and my other two remaining associates.

Special Agent Sader and the DA stayed in the background while we were separated, taken in different rooms by groups of policemen; the PPD vented their frustration and grief for their fallen comrades, mixing interrogating and beating, trying to get confessions. The DA and Sader were amazed by how much punishment we were willing to endure.

"You might as well confess. I've told you we have someone connecting your group to the money."

"Fuck all y'all!" Malik's temper raged to fight back.

"What do you need a confession for, if you have someone?" Ra insulted their intelligence.

"Prove it in court!"

"Strike up the jury!"

"True justice will prevail." We all were passionate to our commitment to each other.

We hadn't been given a call or allowed any interaction with each other. They; Sader and Jurroda had hidden us, trying to divide us with propaganda.

"They're saying you're the master mind. You planned these robberies when you all were in prison together."

Mixing public information with guesses, asking and telling, knowing but not knowing.

"You're violating my rights!" Then a left hook knocked me out.

We knew they had to arraign us or risk their whole case being thrown out. Three weeks later they arraigned us and our bruises from the beatings were still visible. Once in the presence of the public we had some leverage.

It was the first time the five of us had seen each other in 22 days. Instead of distinguished looking, our appearance was distorted, a distraction from our true character. But with a haircut, shave, bath and fresh clothes our appearance could be reconciled. We looked weak, but we weren't broken. The look in our eyes showed unity. We didn't speak, it was too many unknowns in the holding cell with us.

The marshals escorted us to the court room. To my surprise MLJ an elite New York defense attorney, the baby brother of a friend from another world, that I didn't want to return to; MLJ, Myles Langston James, represented all of us. Not guilty pleas were entered by all of us.

"Your Honor, my clients are requesting bail."

"Mr. District attorney, your views regarding bail?"

"Your Honor, I suggest bail be denied due to the violent nature of the crimes, and the penalty being faced. There are four deaths in this case. And the government is seeking the death penalty when the defendants are found guilty.

"Your honor, my clients are innocent until proven guilty, and are entitled to bail."

A soul penetrating eye contact, then the mallet fell. "Bail is set at two million dollars, per defendant. Trial is to start in 21 days."

I thought it was the same as no bail. The marshals were approaching.

"Man, they have nothing on us. This is a witch hunt. Tell Double R, thanks for sending you."

"We'll talk in a little while."

I, we thought he was speaking of an attorney visit, but when the marshals took us from the holding cell to processing, then dressed us out, we were dumbfounded.

MLJ and my wife and son were outside the court building. I could see the love, anger and pain in my wife's face as she embraced me. A kiss, then she gave me a chance to pick up my son while she spoke to us as a group.

"If either of you run, we lose the company." She then took CB2's hand and left. "I'm working your shift."

Courtney' s demeanor showed she was mad, but still had my back. She'd established a dummy hedge fund to cloak the money, so our business couldn't be used as a motive. She slept in CB2's room that night.

The next morning, in my office at the factory, MLJ had assembled us, "I've gone over the discovery and the circumstantial evidence they're trying to use to link you to the bank robberies. It isn't enough to warrant a grand jury indictment let alone a conviction."

"What about their witness?"

"They mention a witness, but this so-called witness hasn't given any statements. This witness didn't testify to the grand jury. There's nothing in the discovery that shows a witness exist. There is no proof of a witness. The only prayer the DA has is a witness. ... There's no other physical or any other kind of evidence linking either of you to the crimes. I've gone head to head with Jurroda before. He will do anything to get a win."

"What do you suggest we do?"

"Allow me to handle the legal ends, and you tie up all your loose ends. I have a meeting I can't miss."

I saw MLJ out, then returned to the others who were discussing Prince.

"The youngster has to be the witness. No one else has an idea of what we were doing."

We all had million-dollar life insurance policies, so it was death before dishonor, plus our families would be taken care of, so that eliminated our fallen comrade's wife.

"The youngster's thorough. The DA is fishing, reaching for shit to divide us or make us show our hands." Ra was going to bat for Prince.

"I don't know. Everyone saw him when they picked us up the first time, but he wasn't in the cell with none of us."

"I like the youngster, but I don't honestly know how he'll handle this type of pressure." Malik's expression was more uncertain than his words.

I'd absorbed all of the opinions, "Can anyone of us with a hundred percent certainty say the youngster won't turn into a rat? Ra?" No one spoke up, "But we know for certain what will keep him from turning into a rat."

All of us were married with children and had lived behind the wall before, and neither of us wanted to give up our life and family to die behind a wall. It showed in our eyes, our commitment to our unity.

"Ra, it was your decision to start the transaction, so make the appropriate arrangement to end it."

CHAPTER 23

PRECIOUS

Codes of personal responsibility in an ideal world would work toward the common goal of benefiting the client and the seller. But when you make something routine change is inevitable in all aspects.

Chub and I were parked across the street from the park, watching as one of my transactions transpired.

"The word on the street is there's ten-grand on Prince's head. Word is, he's snitching."

"My brother isn't a muthafuckin' snitch! Put it out there, it's fifty grand on the head of whoever the fuck started this lie!"

Chub got out of the vehicle, dressed like a homeless person, then retrieved the back pack from the dumpster. I tried to call the house to check on my brother, but his number was disconnected.

Chub returned, checking to make sure no one was watching, then got back into the SUV.

I checked the backpack to find the money that was inside was knots of newspaper wrapped with a hundred-dollar bill.

West was shadowing the dude who had dropped the backpack and picked up the present. The guy was heading toward a car. I called West's cell. "He's playing games. Get my shit!"

West followed the guy to a home. An attractive woman greeted the guy at the door. Through the front window West could see two more guys and a new born baby. West called my cell "The dumb muthafucka went straight home. It's three dudes, a woman and a baby."

"Do you need us to come help?"

"Naw, just give him a call in 30 seconds. I've got it."

The woman looked out the window, then closed the blinds.

West cautiously went to the front door and rang the doorbell. West had a 9mm in both hands and two in the small of his back. He could hear the sound of the cellphone ringing inside of the house getting closer to the door.

My distorted voice was on the dude's phone. "You're dead, you know that right. You stupid muthafucka!"

"Fuck you! Come and get me!"

"You're dead and everybody in your house is dead! I just wanted you to know this!"

Fear registered on the dude's face once he'd opened the door half of the way, realizing he hadn't checked to see who it was.

The fire exploded from the end of the 9mm.

The two men inside were reaching for their guns on the table when West stepped over the dude's body, shooting both guns, emptying the clips into both men. West then quickly grabbed the guns from the small of his back, just in time to shoot the woman before she could raise the AK 47 in his direction.

Without a second thought West snatched the work off the coffee table and the three backpacks around the table.

The baby was screaming when West left the house. Once on the road, West called me, "The baby is alone."

I used one of my throwaway phones to call 911 so someone would hurry and comfort the baby."

.....

You don't have to be a man, to be the man. My function was packed to capacity. The VIP section had thinned out, a few guys here and there were spread out. An older but fly guy who I'd seen with Shey, several times, was two tables away from June and my table. Chub was sitting at the table between us and the guy, so it looked as if Chub could've been the older guy's body guard.

A handsome but shady looking guy entered the section. Both Chub and I recognized him as my customer that had found a better deal and had stopped dealing with me.

Black uninvitedly sat at the older guy's table, "Look, I know I backed away from you, but my people got murked. So, let's crank back up."

"What are you talking about? Do I know you?"

"I know how discreet you are, but this lick is too much money. It's that big payday, big enough for both of us to get out of the game."

The older guy got up and left Black sitting. I and Chub had both been eavesdropping. We then made eye contact and Chub stood blocking Black's way. "He doesn't want to speak with you. I suggest you go about your business." Then stepped aside allowing Black to leave, thinking the older guy was his boss.

...

June was doing her best to arouse me, but I was trying my best to study for my examines. June's playful antics; tickling my feet, blowing under my nighty, only excited my anger.

"Stop. Stop please. I'm studying. ... Damnit! Didn't I say stop!"

"Come on Precious! You've been studying every night. Let's have some fun."

"Chub! Chub!"

Chub ran up the stairs to my bedroom. "What's what boss lady?"

"Take June to her mother's or wherever she wants to go. Please!"

"You're putting me out?"

"Yes. I can't study with you here. Go, Go!"

June was hurt and pissed, angrily packing her things in silence.

She tearfully directed Chub to her boyfrlend's apartment building. "Let me out here."

"I'll take your things up for you."

"No, I'll manage."

Her boyfriend was in the middle of making ecstasy suckers when she used her key to open his door."

"You're crying?"

"Hell naw!"

"What happened?"

"The bitch kicked me out! Help me with this shit"

"Don't come here taking it out on me because you're mad at her. Is she in the dope game?"

"I don't know!"

"Well, what the hell is she doing to eat the way she is?"

"She's smart! She's promoting!"

"Bitch shut up and finish making this shit! Your dumbass has been with her all this time and didn't learn shit! I should kick your dumbass out too!"

.....

Alone again. I realized how much I missed my family. I started thinking about what Prince had said. I drove by the gym, then parked across the street and watched my brothers and Phoenix through the windows. Crying to myself, missing them, needing them; thinking more and more about I was a part of something whole, something bigger than myself. Thoughts of getting out of the game and rejoining my family.

Phoenix and Prince noticed me, so I drove off.

...

I used my distorted voice to call Black. He was excited to hear from me. I directed him to the Greyhound bus station's bathroom to a phone behind the toilet. As soon as he picked up the phone it rang and he heard my distorted voice again.

"How many?"

"20, but it can't be any mission impossible shit. It's not my money and this brother ain't willing to let me handle this without him by my side. So, we're gonna have to do this one the old fashion way."

"When do you need them?"

"He's a southern cat. He's gonna need a few days to drive up."

"When?"

"Four days."

"All right." I wasn't comfortable with the indecisiveness, but I was willing to risk it to get out.

I went all in, to cash out. Every penny I had saved, even my college fund account. Flacco had been excited to hear 20, and even more to see the cash.

"Marry me?"

"Count the money so we can go."

"I'll give you the world."

We both watched his female assistant load the money into counting machine.

"I don't want the world."

"I'll give you whatever you want."

"No thank you."

Once his assistant nodded the amount was correct, I hit send on my cell and both Chub and West entered the room and removed the suitcases.

...

Change can surprise you only if you don't expect it; I was looking for it. I'd completed my six week examines and was feeling good about myself, June was eyeing me from across the hall. She was stunning. "I like your new hairstyle. It looks good on you."

"Thanks."

"I'm sorry, but I had to study. C'mon back home. I miss you."

"You're just like a nigga. Treat me like shit, but as soon as you want some, you want me back."

I started laughing, not at her, but at myself, at what I'd been doing wrong. I walked off, and she stood there dumbfounded in the middle of the hallway.

I went home and wrote on my sports blog.

CHAPTER 24

PRINCE

The hood has a distinct justice system; established rules.

The majority of the Blacks and Mexicans at Saint Mary's high were on scholarship and from the hood, so I was catching stares at school, and the brothers from the football team left the weight room when I entered.

My usual crew ostracized me in the cafeteria like I had a plague. Then to top everything, the entire class watched as the assistant principal entered and passed me a note. I tried to hide my emotions because I knew everyone was watching.

Campbell was outside the class room waiting on me when the bell rang, ending school. "I wasn't trying to play you. My dad didn't know we were dating. I didn't know I would start feeling like this about you. I'm sorry I didn't tell you who my daddy was, but I knew somehow you would react the way you have."

"But since you thought I needed him, you thought I wouldn't trip."

She followed me to the bus stop, "I was only trying to help you. I'm human! I made a mistake. I make mistakes. Can we kiss and make up?" She looked so cute about to cry.

"I can use a friend, and a ride. I've got to go to the middle school. Don't ask. I don't know why."

.....

Phihiem and Phoenix were outside the school, mean mugging some teenaged boys who had black eyes and burst lips. Someone had gotten the best of them. I knew the two elderly ladies and the young woman who were exiting the building behind the boys.

"Hey Mrs. Ross, Mrs. Cox. What's up Anita?"

"These boys getting into grown folks' mess. How's your mama and Precious?"

"Precious is Precious. But mom is still fighting for her life."

Mrs. Ross was eye balling me like I disgusted her.

"Well, I'ma say it. We're praying for Phyllis, but whatever you've gotten yourself in ain't a reason to put the law on CB'em. He's helping the neighborhood a whole lot more than you are." She worked at the factory so her opinion was set in stone.

"Mrs. Ross, I have respect for you, so I'm asking you not to ever scar my character again. I haven't put the law on anyone."

"Well, that's what they're saying."

"Who! Who is they? Take me to one person saying I'm snitching, and I promise you he's lying!"

"Baby I believe you."

"Thank you, Mrs. Cox. How about you Anita?"

"Time will tell. Y'all c'mon if y'all want a ride. I'm late for my shift as is!"

.....

Principle Ellery was in his office with Pharaoh who had a black eye. Principle Ellery spoke once seeing my reaction to Pharaoh's bruises. "He's fine, compared to the other three. ... Prince, I don't care for this display of violence. And Pharaoh won't tell me what's this is concerning. I'm suspending him for three days, and I'm making a suggestion off the records; all four, five of you need to sign up for therapy. Where's Precious? ... You all, allow me to have a word alone with Prince? ..."

Once the door closed behind my brothers and sister, Principle Ellery's entire demeanor changed, "I live in this community. I know what this is over. You've boxed yourself in a tight corner!"

"I'm not involved in any bank licks, and I'm not snitching."

"You're still boxed in."

"I'm a boxer. If all else fail, I'll box my way out." It was ironic so I laughed.

"This isn't a joking matter."

"You're telling me?"

.....

The city was split; half was behind me and the rest were for Cuda Bay. All my vending machines had been vandalized and destroyed. I'd changed the house's phone number due to the death threats and harassing calls. People either stared or waved when they saw me. I had money to pay the mortgage and household bills for a few months, but that meant I wouldn't be able to pay anything towards my mother's hospital bill. I'd become frustrated trying to think of a way to bring in an income.

...

I was sparring when Malik and Ra entered the gym. I stopped and focused on them. I was raging on the inside but I appeared calm as I left the ring, taking the tape off my gloves. They had to behind the rumors. They saw I was approaching but ignored me, as if to start their workout. My rage went to a different level. I hit Ra with a combination that put him on his back. I was about to stomp him until Malik grabbed me from behind. Pharaoh immediately socked Malik in the ear, making him release me. I collared Ra, dropping haymakers on him until the entire gym was pulling me off of him, and separating Pharaoh and Phihiem from Malik.

Malik was banged up but could walk. "You muthafuckas are dead! You heard me!" Shouting to the top of his lungs as he dragged a punch-drunk Ra out of the gym.

Nubs was holding the door open, "What happened to all that love and soul brother shit? I knew y'all was some shit when you started preaching it. Get your ass out of my gym before I kick your ass until both of my shoes are shitty!"

Since my session ended early, we'd stopped by the local market, instead of waiting until the next day. I hadn't taken Malik's words as an idle threat, but I figured with as many people that were in the gym, he wouldn't act too quickly on his promise.

We had two push carts full of groceries and had made it a half of a block from the store when I spotted a car following us at a slow pace. I picked up the pace, as did my brothers and Phoenix – suspiciously looking around then at me for an answer why.

"When I say run, we're going to sprint to our block."

"I'm not a track star. I'm not running from anybody!"

"This won't be a fist fight. All we have to do is get to our block. J and Rod will be on point."

"No they won't. They think we're soft, since you made us skip out on midnight madness."

We heard the motor of the car revving.

"Run!"

"What about our food!"

I snatched up Phoenix, carrying her while running and shouting, "Leave it!"

We all saw the nozzle of an AK47 sticking out of the car window.

"We're not going to make it!" Phoenix was right.

"Go to Mrs. Cox's!"

Pharaoh and Phihiem got to the door first, knocking and pounding and yelling, "Mrs. Cox! Come open the door!"

We didn't have time to wait. As soon as I got up the stairs, I kicked the door off the hinges in one try. Bullets busted the windows as we ran through the house to the back door. Luckily no one was home.

We jumped the fence to the next yard, then apologized to Mrs. Brown as we entered her back door, scaring her.

"I'm sorry Mrs. Brown, but they're trying to kill us." We didn't stop until we were out of the front door.

I decided it was best to circle back to the gym. Nubs wasn't there, but I had a set of keys and knew the security code to the alarm.

"We've got to do something! We can't let them get away with shooting at us!"

"I want to go home!"

I listened, thinking, seeing the worried fear on the face of Phoenix, while also feeling Pharaoh and Phihiem's anguish.

"We can't, not yet. You all stay here, and don't go near the windows. And don't turn on any lights."

"Where are you going?" From a pleading concerned Phoenix.

"To make sure we can go home."

"I'm going with you! I'm older enough to clap back!"

"Me too!"

"No-ooo! No-ooo! To all of this! If you do something stupid they'll split us up. We've got to be smart!" Phoenix was hysterical but rational.

I hugged her while trying to explain, "I'll rather see you all in foster homes than see you dead."

I kissed her forehead, then gave my brothers two hard pounds before I left weighing my options while sneaking around the neighborhood.

Members of the study hall were hanging out with some of the guys from my block. I went through the back door to get into my home. The inside had been trashed, spray painted. Rat and snitch were written on the walls and furniture, which was also ripped and broken. The mattresses and pillows were cut open, Clothes bleached. The cash I had at the house was gone. I threw the mattress across the room furious, then went to the backyard and dug up an AK 47 with two clips and a mask.

...

Cuda Bay lived in the hood, the nicest section, but still in the hood, in walking distance from my home.

The moon was high and bright. I could see Cuda Bay and his family, eating dinner through the front window of their home. No one expected it. The ones that knew my dark side were dead, so who would expect I would kill or die for my family. I wasn't afraid to die.

CHAPTER 25

CUDA BAY

The value I'd given the situation was much too low. I'd grossly underestimated the seriousness. I was playing when I shouldn't have been. I was in my comfort zone, enjoying giving CB2 his bath when my wife stepped to the entrance of the bathroom with tears in her eyes.

"What's wrong? Was it Ra at the door?"

A hand somewhat pushed her into the bathroom, and I could see the AK 47 to the back of her head. Then I saw into the eyes of the manifestation of nothing and everything, blackness, the cold stare of Prince.

"I'm not a snitch. If they had something on me, I would lay down and take mine. From my understanding, they don't have anything on anyone!"

"Why are you in my damn house! Involving my family in this!"

"Because you have a hit out on me! And someone tried to cash in on it while I was with my family! Involving my family! Endangering my family!"

The shouting echoed in the bathroom, plus seeing the tears running down his mother's face, scared CB2 to tears. "Daddy don't let him kill mommy."

"I'm here to set the record straight; I'm not a snitch and this is my only warning. The next time my family is endangered, yours become extinct!"

He could've taken something much more valuable than my freedom; my family. The look in his eyes showed the strength and courage to kill, but instead he backed away, leaving us in the bathroom.

CHAPTER 26

PRINCE

Campbell was at the gym. She and my brothers and Phoenix were relieved to see me. Phoenix had called her after only reaching Precious' voice mail. Pharaoh and Phihiem's eyes were asking what happened.

"Things will back to normal before the morning."

"Why don't you ask my father for help? He has the power ..."

"I know what your father is."

"My dad isn't the one shooting at you! My dad isn't the bad guy."

Her father was mob related, and I felt like I would be selling my soul to the devil if I asked him for help. Plus I didn't want to give up my dreams of winning a gold-medal in the Olympics.

"Just take us home please?"

"I will not! I've been by your place. They're waiting on you. I'll take you to a hotel, but I'm not taking you home. My dad can help. Don't let your pride put you guys in harm's way."

"I don't have money for a hotel room."

"I've got you."

"What if it takes longer than expected?"

"I've got you."

The hotel was so far away from the city, I thought we were going to New York.

Campbell's mother and step father were in Seattle, giving a seminar, so her staying over at the hotel wasn't a problem.

The pizza and pay preview, plus the excitement of the day had exhausted Phoenix and my brothers. Campbell had gotten two rooms; one for the guys and the other for Phoenix and herself.

Campbell and I left Phoenix asleep in my bed. Campbell's passion was so intense it was hard to tell if she was grateful I was there, or afraid it would be our last time.

My mental alarm clock awakened me. I laid there contemplating what to do. I felt boxed in, limited of choices. I had to, needed to think differently.

Campbell shook off the idea of going to school. She was snoring when I asked to use her ride.

I drove around thinking, punching every option a million times in my mind's eye until only one remained standing.

Campbell rolled over once I sat on the bed. "I know the perfect deli, that's not too far from here."

"First I want you to call your father. I would like a meeting with him as soon as possible."

.....

Just as in boxing, it is in life; preparation is key if you hope to operate well under pressure. Mr. Bosco had cancelled his flight. We met at his downtown NYC office, in an impressive huge conference room. A team of suits and two dresses were assembled. I knew they'd been talking about me, decisions had been made and my presence was only a formality. Their look, their style, their silence. I could see they couldn't imagine how stressful it was asking for help, because people with power don't place themselves in situations where they don't have the upper hand. I understood my lack of education, experience and expertise at negotiating put me at a clear disadvantage. So once I'd decided to seek help from Mr. Bosco, I had stopped by a friend of my mother's who was a lawyer; she'd helped and prepped me on my rights so I would be better prepared, going into the all-important meeting that could determine my very life, my family's future.

Mr. Bosco was frank and to the point, "I don't have all day. Here's your contract. It's legit. The highest percentage I've dealt out to someone who has never thrown a professional punch. When you sign it, I'm placing your name in the pool for the championship tournament. I hope you're ready. Flip will be your trainer."

Brackets were setup on the board, two different sets.

"Whoa, you're moving too fast. Here's our contract." I extended the contract my lawyer friend had typed up for me. "I'm here, giving you the opportunity to be my exclusive promotor. I don't need a trainer or a manager. And I have my PR personnel."

"Who do you think you are, coming into my office with this smug attitude!"

"Daddy!"

"Mr. Bosco, I'm going to be the heavy weight champion of the world!"

Mr. Bosco was gritting on Campbell who had the same stern expression. He broke weak for her, and used a finger to signal his staff out of the room. "... How can you be the champ if you're dead?"

"I've handled that situation."

Doubt registered, "How?"

"I made an uninvited house call."

He was surprised, but impressed, "You just walked up to his door?" I only nodded. "Jesus son! Is he still breathing?"

"Yes. He listened to reasoning."

"And you believed him? You should've ..." He stopped himself. "... Princess, take them to the lounge for a snack, please? While I discuss details with Prince."

We all caught the irony in Campbell's pet name and my name. His facial expression kicked into father mode.

"Mr. Bosco, I really don't want them out of my sight."

"Son, this is my building. They're, you all are safer here than anywhere in the world. ... Princess, give us a moment."

I nodded to my brothers and sister to go with Campbell. Once we were the only two in the office, the raised hand of Mr. Bosco stopped me from speaking, "Why didn't you finish what you went there to do?"

"I couldn't get away with it."

"If you get the opportunity to get away with it?"

"If he breaks our agreement, I've have no choice."

No one mentioned the terms death or kill.

"Do you think he's going to keep his end of the agreement?"

"He's a smart man, and a good man. I can understand his point of view, but I'm not a snitch."

"Do you trust him?"

"The only thing I trust is the sun to rise and set."

Mr. Bosco flipped through the pages of the contract, "I'm not going to sign this until my lawyers check it out. My daughter is going to Yale."

"I know. I'm helping her get there. I'm tutoring her in chemistry. Campbell is in my corner and I appreciate her. I wouldn't do anything to hold her back from reaching her dreams."

"What are your dreams?"

"The heavy weight champion, then become a lawyer. But my ultimate goal is to be a supreme justice." My cell rang and I saw it was the hospital. "I'm sorry Mr. Bosco, but this is the hospital calling. ... Thank you for calling. I'm on my way. ... Mr. Bosco, I have to leave."

"Is it more important than your future?"

"It's pertaining to my mother who is in a coma and might not have a future."

.....

The situation at the hospital wasn't as dreadful as I thought. Once we got to ICU nurse Pottier, the one who'd called, was seated at my mother's beside holding my mother's hand. "I've always admired your ambition and strong will ..." She stopped once the administrative director and the doctor arrived with policemen and security guards.

Nurse Pottier's attitude changed and she quickly left the room.

"Mr. Battle, I'm glad you're here. We're transferring your mother to Mercy Central in the morning."

"Why?"

"There's nothing else we can do for her. Her brain activity will be down to none within weeks."

Phoenix immediately started crying. The doctor and the director both stepped back when I stood from my mother's bedside. My mother's eyes darted to my movement, her hand still had a grasp of mine; she made me stop.

"State the truth, the real reason why you want to transfer our mother!"

"Mr. Battle it's to your financial benefit, with the accumulating cost of your mother being at this establishment."

"I'm not authorizing any transfer!"

"You don't have to."

I was furious, but I had to think, to be rational. "I'm going to pay the bill! Don't transfer her!"

"The decision has been made."

"Get the hell out of our sight! Let us visit our mother in peace!"

I'd made sure the lawyer put a signing bonus into the promotional contract with Mr. Bosco, but I didn't know how long before he would agree. I needed money at that moment. If it was the end for my mother, I wasn't going to allow her to spend her last moments in a county hospital. Only one person could understand and could help, but to ask Precious for money would contradict everything I'd been preaching, but I had no choice. I was boxed in.

Precious answered her cell on the first ring. I didn't give her time to say anything. "I need you to come to the hospital. ... Can it be quicker than that? ... Where are you? ... I'll be there in five minutes."

Campbell volunteered to stay at the hospital with my brothers and sister, to do whatever they could to stop the administration if they tried to transfer my mother before I returned.

CHAPTER 27

PRECIOUS

The feeling I had wasn't natural. I was anxious to get the transaction over. I had a throw-away cell phone, which I'd connected to a device that distorted my voice. Black was on the line, I had given him the directions.

"... I know what you look like. I'll get your attention when you get here." I ended the call and got out of the SUV. West and I were already at the bookstore. "Stay here. Just in case he tries something."

West got back into the vehicle. I had Chub posted at the location of the work. I was ready to get it over, but I was also prepared for the unexpected.

I was positioned in the coffee shop lounge of the bookstore so I saw when Prince arrived. He parked next to Black's Benz, who had only pulled up seconds before Prince. Black had arrived 30 minutes early. He and the fellow in the car with him seemed to be discussing something while scanning the bookstore and the parking lot.

Prince paused when he got out of Campbell's Benz, then came into the store looking puzzled. I had a new book by Walter Mosely. Prince took it as he sat, playfully reading it, then gave it back. "I turned pro. I want you to be a part of my team, as my PR manager. This way you can give up the game, and we can be a family again."

"Why now?"

"A lot of reasons. But they're trying to transfer mom to Mercy Central, if I can't pay the medical expenses."

"I'm all in. But I'll have it after I handle this last deal. ... So yes, I'll accept your offer to be your PR personnel. We can all go out for dinner tonight and celebrate."

Prince noticed my eyes dart toward the entrance; Black and the fellow were coming inside. Prince focused in on the fellow.

"You go ahead and leave, and I'll be by the hospital when I finish this."

I was about to raise my hand to get Black's attention when Prince grabbed and kissed me on the mouth.

Prince mumbled under his breath, "That's the police! I remember his face from the precinct."

"Thank you, but they don't know what I look like or who I am. Let's go."

We both made eye contact with Black and the agent as we left the bookstore. I couldn't allow my anger to cloud my judgement, Prince needed me, my mother needed us, and all my money was tied up in 20 kilos of heroin. Prince walked me to the SUV, listening to my instruction.

"... Just be ready to give a press release in an hour. I'll email your speech."

I put together Prince's speech While Chub and I waited in the parking lot, waiting until Black and the agent gave up. An unmarked police car pulled to the bookstore and Black and the agent went their separate ways. We followed Black to his apartment. I stayed in the vehicle. Chub caught the elevator's door before it closed. There were three other tenants aboard. Chub got off on the same floor as Black, but went in the opposite direction as if looking for an apartment, then doubled back; Black was unlocking his door when he looked up.

"Do you know which apartment is Sasha's? Big ass, pretty face sister." Chub continued approaching Black.

"I'm not sure. It's a lot of sexy sisters on this floor."

"I've got a picture." Chub acted as if he was going for his wallet, but instead pulled out his nine, "Open the door you snitching-ass bitch."

"You've got me fucked up! I ain't no snitch!"

Chub slapped him with the gun into the apartment, then closed the door. "If you lie to me I'm gonna kill you." Then took Black's gun.

Black noticed Chub putting both guns in the small of his back.

Black quickly got to his feet and flicked out his knife. "So what I tried to set you up? A muthafucka did it to me?" Then leaped at Chub with the knife.

Chub threw a straight-jab to Black's throat, that made Black drop the knife and grab his own throat.

Chub patiently picked up the knife, "Let me help you breathe." Then sliced Black's throat.

Chub held him down while pulling Black's tongue through the gaping hole in Black's neck.

Chub stood there and watched Black drown in his own blood.

CHAPTER 28

PRINCE

When major decisions had to be made, when one of us needed help, we became one, regardless of our difference, we knew we could depend on one another, because we were family.

I hadn't quite memorized the speech, but I was pleased with it.

It relayed the message of need and hope to those who could best help. Precious' talents never ceased to amaze me.

I was standing in front of the emergency room as Precious had advised, when all the major local television news vans started arriving with complete camera teams. They all rushed to interview me.

"Why have you chosen to bypass the Olympics and turn pro, giving up your lifelong dream?!"

"Many don't know that my mother, my sister and a close friend of the family were in a car- jacking that killed our close friend, left my mother in a coma from being shot in the head, and my sister barely escaped with her life after also being shot in the head and left for dead. ... I've applied for aid from the city, the county, the state and the federal government. What little assistance I have received isn't enough to cover the medical cost."

Precious had planned it perfect so that Pharaoh, Phihiem and Phoenix exited the hospital and came to my side.

"... These are my brothers and one of my sisters. My mother raised us to be fighters. I'm not asking for donations. I know times are hard. What I am asking, we are asking; is for you to call, write, email, fax, text or walk up to the administration of this hospital and ask them to give my mother, Phelisa Battle, a fair fight. A fighting chance, and not pull the plug or transfer her. Don't throw the towel in. I will pay the hospital bill, every cent of it. This is why I'm moving up to the rank of professional fighter, to meet the responsibilities of a son and a big brother."

 For a few seconds the crowd was respectfully silent, then "Who is your manager? ... Who is your first victim? ... Are you going into the pool to face the Hammer?"

"I'll fight anyone worthy of fighting at anytime, but right now, I'm fighting to support my family. Thanks for your support."

.....

As we approached the gym I felt like I had betrayed Nubs, Since my first fight he'd preached gold metal. The press had beaten us to the gym, crowding, blocking my way into the gym. After I repeated my family responsibility speech; asking for support, we pushed our way inside.

Nubs had his good liquor out. He was in a manic depress mode. His ice bucket was empty, so instead of pouring liquor into his glass, he turned up the bottle.

"I don't believe you kicked everything to the curb. Years! I know I ain't the father figure, but at least I thought you looked at me as family. The Olympic committee okayed you. You had made the team. But puff, gone!"

"The fight switched up on us. I had to change our strategy."

"Kid you can't beat death!"

"I know that! But money can prolong it!"

"Your mom is suffering. Why prolong it?"

"Because I'm not 18! So if they pull the plug or somehow my mom dies being transferred, Phoenix, Phihiem and Pharaoh will go to a foster home: Because I'm not legally old enough to have custody of them! So, since I didn't know of a sponsor willing to pay an one point three million dollars and still rising medical bill, I turned pro! If you can't understand, then you don't need to be in my corner!"

·····

For the next couple of days my appeal got national attention: CNN's coverage of the hospital, and ESPN's coverage of me turning pro, which brought massive advertisement of me and Nubs' Gym, and a stay on my mother's transfer. Membership more than tripled at the gym. Donations flooded the hospital.

News reporters, journalists and opportunists started camping out in front of our house, following me on my morning runs, even when I dropped Phoenix and the guys off at school.

Campbell had used her black card to get us all new wardrobes, since every item of clothing in the house had been ruined. She never asked for anything in return. My love for her had grown, so I felt really bad about her playing the background when the cameras and the reporters were around. She hadn't complained, but I could tell it bothered her. We weren't a secret, but no one spoke of it, not even at school until Brooke stopped me in the hallway by my locker. She was teary eyed, hurt, confused and mad. I guess she'd reached her boiling point when she read or heard of my signing bonus and the projected earnings from endorsements. It was difficult looking at her sadness. We'd been each other's first, and had planned our lives out from junior high until death.

"You did it for her?"

"I didn't do it for her. I did it ..."

"I tried to tell you to do it when the mess with mom first happened, but you wouldn't listen! All the years I've had your back, supported you, massaged your aches until my hands ached? I worked and paid for a car that you drove every day! But as soon as you get with her, you turn pro? What about our dreams, our plans?"

"I didn't change our plans, you did! I'm adapting to the changes as they come."

"I should've listened to my sister and lied about being on the pill."

Campbell came up from behind and embraced me, claiming what was hers. "Hey mann! Hi Brooke. Prince, we're going to be late for class."

"Yes, Prince! You don't want to make her wait!"

"Excuse me! Don't talk in code. Speak your mind! Especially if it is pertaining to me." Campbell stepped toward Brooke.

I quickly got between them, "Let's go to class."

"Yeah, take that gold digging bitch to class! But I hope you end up getting schooled by the heifer!"

I had to literally carry Campbell to class.

CHAPTER 29

CUDA BAY

Safety, freedom from worry, a pledge given. Ra had taken his sergeant at arms position to heart, and had detailed an unit of guys to watch over me 24 hours out of the day. At least it kept his mind off of Prince, a debate I was sick of. I was in my office, trying to figure out how to stretch the cash flow; I knew a bank lick would be too risky – then my two body guards escorted Mr. Bosco and his two body guards into my office.

I'd heard Bosco was now silently in Prince's corner.

"Mr. Bosco, as I said; I only have a small window of time open. Please have a seat so we can begin." I could see he was impressed by my operation.

"Thank you for seeing me. I know how precious investments are, and how someone would do anything to keep and protect their investment. Because I feel the same way about my investments. My prize investment at the moment is Prince." He paused, observing for any reaction. "... Before you say anything Mr. Bay. This young man is a man after my heart, and I respect him. And if he breaks my heart I will handle it. With this understood, I hear your sales are good, but you're having a cash flow problem. I'm here to help. I can become your partner or you may prefer a loan."

"At what percentage of interest?"

"Instead of 35 percent, I'll make it 15 percent."

A divine source of karma. I'd kept my word to drop the hit on Prince, and in return a positive way to keep my business afloat to the end of the quarter was made.

CHAPTER 30

PRECIOUS

I'd been laying low, transformed back into the uppity high school girl, while Chub and West had their ears to the street. The police had resurrected Shey's name in the street, but Shey had been so discreet, no one was sure if he was into anything illegal.

Chub and West updated me, "Ray gave us the up that Dora had gotten popped, but used a free get out of jail pass. But he's not sure who Dora gave up."

My mind started spending. Flacco had called me Ms. Shey so many times with Dora present, I knew I was her free get out of jail pass.

"She needs to be silenced."

"She doesn't know what you look like, or where you are or who you are. She doesn't know anything." They both had grown up with Dora, and looked at her at her as family.

"She knows I'm a female, and she knows both of you? That's enough!"

I called Flacco. "... It's me. ... Not really. I'm in a jam. I'm scrapped for cash. I need you to buy these off of me. ... I'm over a barrel. I'll take a lost, but don't try to bleed me to death. ... That's fine. We're on our way."

.....

At Flacco's everything was going as normal until Flacco volunteered to show me the money in his vault. "Let me show you something beautiful."

The door behind his desk actually led into a walk-in vault.

"Why are you showing me this?"

His sinister laughter answered my suspicion. I reached for my cell that was clipped to my side, but he grabbed my wrist and snatched it. "I don't buy dope! My people grow it! Why would you come to my home with dope? How do I know you're not trying to set me up?"

"I answered your questions before I came!" I managed to snatch away from him, then screamed, "Chub! West!"

I tried to defend myself, but Flacco manhandled me, smacking me around, but would grab me before I could reach one of the medieval relics. My vision became blurred as he bent me over the desk, reaching under my skirt, ripping my panties.

I screamed for Chub and West as Flacco started raping me. I could hear the gun shots outside the room. I was seeing double everything. There were two letter openers lying flat on the desk. I reached for the wrong one, then quickly grabbed the right one. I blindly swung hard behind me. The blow stabbed Flacco in the ribs, penetrating a lung. He backed up, gasping for air.

"Don't stop now! I haven't caught mine! What, your sticker stopped working? Okay,

I'll do the sticking then." I stabbed him repeatedly until he was dead.

The shooting had stopped in the other room. I dropped the letter opener in exchange for a sword, off the wall. I then slowly opened the door, Chub and West were the only survivors, but both were badly shot.

Chub and I struggled to put West into the backseat, then I went back into the house and cut off Flacco's dick and balls. I was looking for my cell, which was on the floor in the vault, I wiped down the desk and the letter opener for finger prints, then decided to clean out all the money in the vault.

West died on the way back to Philly. Chub looked closed to death, but continued driving to the house.

"We can split the cash, and you can have the dope. But you need to get out of state, maybe the country."

"You keep it all. I don't think I'm gonna need it. Get out Boss Lady. I love you."

I took the bags of money and dope, then watched as Chub drove off.

Chub paid Dora a visit. Badly shot up and heavily bleeding, he gathered himself outside of the door to Dora's apartment; loading a full clip into his 9mm. Only through will power Chub found the strength to kick the door open.

Dora was nodding, too high to react. Contraband was on the table with a bottle of Hennessey and her glass. She recognized Chub.

"I've been doing this all my life. Five years without it? I couldn't do that. I'll die. I had too. ... I didn't mention you and West."

Chub emptied the clip into her, then sat and drank the last of her glass of Hennessey before dying.

.....

My head was pulsating as if it was going to explode. I couldn't see the numbers on my cell, but somehow I dialed Prince's cell to reach his voice mail. June was the only other person I had left to call. I needed help. I felt like I was dying.

June answered. I could hear a male's voice fussing in the background. "Bitch since you've been back, you're acting like I ain't shit! And my shit ain't good enough!"

"Fuck you! Hello?"

"Please come over, Please? I need you."

"Nigga shut the fuck up so I can hear! Damn! ... Pee baby, what's wrong? Are you hurt?" Her boyfriend tried to snatch the cell. "... I'll be there in fifteen minutes."

June and her boyfriend were dressed to go out, "Bitch you ain't going over there."

"She's hurt and alone. She need me!"

"You love this hoe more than me?"

"Just drop me off on your way to the club."

"Fine!" He was silent the entire ride, just following the direction, then stopped June from getting out of the car, "Introduce me to her?"

"What?"

"Maybe I can help in some way?"

.....

I painfully struggled to open my prescription pain pills, then chased them with XO.

The doorbell rang. It was too agonizing to stand. Half of the way to the door I realized I'd left my 9mm on the coffee table. The pain in my head made me not think straight, so I continued to the door, then peeped out of the window and was relieved to see June. I didn't see her friend; he was to the side.

June saw the blood and panicked while checking me for serious wounds. Her boyfriend stepped in scanning the room, then focusing on the bloody black leather bags.

My vision was blurred but I could tell by his body luggage he was a foe.

"This's Ced. I thought he might could help, since you said you were alone."

"No thank you. I don't need any help. Bye Ced."

"I came to help. You don't have to be afraid of me."

"Do I look like I'm afraid of anything? Now get the fuck out of my house!"

My gun was in clear view, so when I stepped back Ced caught me with a left hook that knocked me on the sofa.

June started screaming at him to "Stop! Get out!"

I had blacked out, then realized I was on the sofa and started digging for my spare under the pillows. He kicked me in the chest, then snatched me off the sofa. June ran at him, then stopped once he drew back to hit her.

To stop me from struggling, he punched me twice, then dragged me over to the bags. Once seeing inside, he became happy as hell, "Jack Pot!"

June was still screaming, until he showed her the money inside the bag, "Shut the fuck up or you can die too, or this could be ours! ... Go sit in the car."

June became silent, then made eye contact with me, and I knew then she was always a friendly foe, even when we were little. She was my friend just to borrow my clothes.

The door closed, and a straight right knocked me on my back. I landed on the floor next to the loveseat. My eyes were swollen closed, but I heard Ced undoing his belt. He saw my hand feeling under the loveseat, then dove on top of me, punching me until I dropped the gun. He then began to rape me.

A clear vase full of colorful marbles was next to us. He was choking me while raping me. I felt the energy draining from my body, but I managed to lift the vase and hit him with it on the side of his face and shoulder. It didn't faze him. He only laughed. His laughter, the idea of him laughing at me, gave me the will, the strength to hit him harder with the vase. It broke, and the marbles went everywhere. Ced was still laughing and choking the life out of me. He hadn't realized I was actually stabbing him in the neck with a piece of the broken glass vase, until he saw his own blood flowing onto my face. He panicked, released my throat and grabbed his own, trying to stop the bleeding. I continued stabbing him until he fell dead to the side of me. I crawled to my cell and incoherently cried to Prince for help before I passed out.

CHAPTER 31

PRINCE

Suffering. I heard it in Precious' voice. Campbell had hurried over after I called. I'd asked her to stay with my brothers and Phoenix. Precious had been mumbling I killed him, so the less people who knew, the better.

The door to the town house was unlocked and Precious was bloody and unconscious when I arrived. I ripped her shirt open, thinking I needed to put pressure on the wound, but there wasn't a wound. Once I realized it was Ced's blood who was lying face down on a rug, soaked with his blood, I took Precious to the shower and washed the blood off of her. She kept gaining consciousness, mumbling, June is in the car. But no one was in any of the cars out front.

I knew I shouldn't have allowed her to go to sleep, but I had to clean up the mess and get rid of the body. The rug took up most of the room. I had to move every piece of furniture to one side, then used the $11,000 rug as a body bag, wrapping it around the body and everything else that had blood on it.

It was a struggle to put the rug into the back of Shey's Land Rover. Precious gained consciousness as I carried her down the stairs toward the door. She was reaching for the bags of money and dope.

"That's not coming with us."

"Please Prince? I've been through too much."

"It's not coming into the house."

The only time we were seen, was pulling off.

Phoenix and the guys and Campbell wanted to take Precious to the hospital. They didn't know the whole story but accepted the idea of nurse Pottier and one of her doctor friends, paying a house call.

I gave Campbell two $10,000 stacks out of one of the black leather bags, "Tell nurse Pottier and the doctor, this is strictly confidential. ... You've got to take a cab to get your ride. It's on Broadway and 12th. I'm sorry. I've got to go." I couldn't wait around.

The sun was rising when I returned home, one hundred percent sure that no one would ever discover the remains of Ced.

CHAPTER 32
CUDA BAY

The chief function of the court, is to interpret and apply the law from whatever source to a given situation. I and my co-defendants were in court. MLJ was representing us. He'd filed a motion for dismal. Our judge's face looked as if he'd been injected with Botox. His expression was blank, mask like, which I took as good or at least he would be neutral, because the DA was furiously shouting his remarks. "... This motion is frivolous! How dare you accuse me of perjury?"

"You had to perjure yourself to get a grand jury indictment against my clients. There's no evidence or hear say throughout the discovery that links my clients to any of the crimes committed. You had to have fabricated a witness, because there's no reported statements or depositions given by anyone. If you didn't perjure yourself why haven't you disclosed the grand jury transcripts? ... Your Honor, district attorney Jurroda would have us believe the grand jury gave an indictment based on three facts; the first being: These men served a federal sentence together at the same prison. The second being: That these men are now members of the same study hall. And the third being; The bags and shoes captured on the surveillance cameras, were made at my client's company."

The judge's voice was deep and penetrating. "District attorney Jurroda, why haven't the defense received a copy of the transcript?"

Jurroda gave a quick grimace at Sader, then gathered his thoughts, "Your Honor, there's a CI, but there's a gag order. Due to the violent nature of the crimes, the CI's life would be in danger."

"Excuse me? Your Honor, the defense wants to know did the witness present an affidavit to the grand jury."

"No your Honor."

"Your Honor, my clients have the right to face their accuser."

"Your Honor, if the prosecution divulges the identity of the CI, they will kill him."

"Your Honor, district attorney Jurroda is violating my clients' 5th and 6th amendments, by withholding evidence. I again move for a dismal."

"District attorney Jurroda, this court is issuing an order compelling the discovery. You have 14 days to give the defense the full discovery of evidence to be used in court to prosecute them. If you do not comply, you will be found in contempt of court, and I will dismiss this case."

CHAPTER 33

PRINCE

The drama in my life was theatrical and kept becoming more complexed. The crowd grew daily, it was a circus show watching me do my suicide sprints on the stairs of the art museum.

Two guys approached me as if they were fans. "You're Prince Battle?"

"Yes."

One then handed me some papers. "You have been served." They were marshals. It was a subpoena to appear in court on November 8th at 11 AM.

At school, Campbell noticed the subpoena in our locker. "You need a lawyer?"

"I have one."

It was cool, the way she dealt with drama. She didn't freak out or shy away. I guess growing up the daughter of Frank Bosco had made her a ride or die chick.

"What did your lawyer say?"

"If they had anything on me, it would be an indictment instead of a subpoena."

"Have you discussed this with my dad?"

"This doesn't pertain to your father. Only me and my family."

"What about me?"

"This is something I have to handle."

My day went as normal as the unexpected. Nubs had me studying film on the top fifty fighters of the world. He and Phoenix were both pointing out tell tell-signs of the boxers' give away moves before they threw a certain punch, while I tried to keep up writing notes on each fighter.

That night in bed the pressure crushed me, I could easily calculate formulas, comprehend language art, predict boxers' moves, but every decision I'd made regarding my family's wellbeing had rippled into making things worse. It was things I didn't know, that people expected me to already know or learn very quickly. I was living, which was learning.

CHAPTER 34

CUDA BAY

Our ethical standards apply to every aspect of life. What in good conscience ought to be done?

Jurroda had given us full disclosure of the discovery and the names of six witnesses and their signed affidavits. Prince's name was one, but no statement had been given by him. Of the other five witnesses, four were federal inmates willing to testify to anything to get a sentence reduction. The last witness, a M.I.T. graduate, with so many degrees it was unreal.

Since the Black population of Philly was in the upper 70 percent, Jurroda knew the pool of jurors would reflect it, so he motioned to change vendors, which was denied,

Juror selection went in our favor. The jury was selected and sworn in.

When the trial started, it was hard watching guys I had ate with and studied with, take the stand against me. These guys were supposedly the thorough of the thorough. The study hall in prison we'd started, required paperwork for entry. Neither of them had snitching in their jackets. Time had weakened them, and each still had a decade to do before being released, but there's no excuse for snitching. They'd done their own crime, reaped the benefits, but couldn't endure the punishment.

"... He always had several options, back up plans. ... The main option would always be legitimate, but his safety net to finance his projects if all else failed, would always be a bank lick. ... He's very convincing. He's a genius. He charms you with words until you see his picture mixed in with your dreams. He's a master mind. He can convert radical Christians and Muslims to science. ... He sent me money monthly. He wanted me to come work for him upon my release. Be his muscle on collections. Like I did in prison for him when he ran a store and loan sharked."

They all basically said the same thing and gave well-rehearsed performances until MLJ crossed examined them. "... I don't care if everything you have said is the truth or a lie. My question is; what personal information do you have that connects the defendants to the present crimes they're being charged with committing?"

Speechless, mute, wordless and soundless.

"Your Honor, I move we imply the witness' silence to be incompetence or lack of personal knowledge of anything connecting the defendants to the present charges."

Jurroda stood objecting. "Your Honor!"

"District attorney Jurroda it should be your witness speaking, not you. Sit down. ... Sir? Do you understand the question?"

"Yes your Honor."

"Well then answer it."

"None. ..."

"No I do not. ..."

"No. ..."

"No. ..."

"Only one more question. Why are you a witness in a criminal case you know nothing of?" Again, silence as they looked down, knowing but not wanting to admit; the DA had used a time cut as cheese to draw out the rat within them. "I'll answer the question for you. You're testifying for a time deduction! ..."

Jurroda stood screaming, "Objection! Objection!"

But MLJ continued over him. "... Instead of having a remaining sentence of 130 months, you now only have 24 months to serve before you are released!"

"Mr. James if you don't have proof of this accusation I'll declare this case a miss trial!" Banging his mallet hushing the crowd.

MLJ looked at his watch, then at the white woman who was approaching him with a smile and a folder. "I do your Honor. The defense would like to submit the plea agreements, signed by the witnesses and the U.S. district attorney Jurroda, as exhibit A." Then gave the copies to the judge, the bailiff and Jurroda.

The judge nodded, and the bailiff passed the copies to the jurors. MLJ had known if he'd submitted the plea agreements without tricking the judge into asking for proof, the evidence wouldn't had been allowed.

Jurroda read the disapproval on the jurors' faces as they scanned the copies. "Your Honor, the government requests a recess."

"Granted until 9:45 AM tomorrow!"

MLJ had brilliantly revealed the ruthless tactics of the government and had solidified the community behind me.

The crowd waited in front of the court building, blocking the streets to show their support. I was amazed by the show of unity.

.....

9:30 AM the courtroom was filled-to-capacity. A contraption had been assembled in front of the jury bench. It looked like an electronic science project.

The jury came out, then the judge immediately called court to order. Dr. Escant, the founder of Image Scan, a company contracted by the government in the war on terror. Dr. Escant was sworn in as an expert witness to analyze what was being held as physical evidence; the surveillance footage from the banks which was fed into the machine, coded to breakdown the digital imaging and measure the images by stress points of movements; computing the actual height, weight, gender and age, detecting abnormalities in the limbs and attitude. The doctor okayed the use of his camera phone, then recorded Jurroda walking from his desk to the rail of the jury bench. The doctor connected the cell to the machine, then downloaded the recording.

"Mr. Jurroda is 6' 3" 241.6 pounds, a 47-year-old male, with a sore right knee, and is a little stressed."

"An old college basketball injury, and the stress comes with the job." Smiling, impressed by the psychic show. The jury was also.

Dr. Escant analyzed the footage from the surveillance, calculating, pinpointing details of all my co-defendants.

Jurroda then made a request, "Your Honor the government submits the defendants' height, weight, age and gender as proof of the accuracy."

The judge and MLJ's eyes met and had a silent conversation before the judge granted the request.

Jurroda sat and MLJ stood, "Very impressive credentials in front and behind your name."

"Thank you."

"I'm a people person. I'm inclined to make my judgement after I get to know the person, not by looking at them."

"Your Honor, irrelevant. What does this ..."

"You're right. Dr. Escant, if someone emails me, could your machine still work its magic?"

"Yes."

"Your Honor, I would like to perform a demonstration on behalf of the defense, using Dr. Escant expertise?"

"Your Honor, the accuracy has been determined!"

"Proceed Mr. James."

The footage was of a masked figure, familiarly dressed identical to the bank robbers; designer suit, shirt, tie and shoes and gloves, pacing in a public restroom. Dr. Escant analyzed the digital information with relative ease and quickly.

"Five feet and eight inches. 143.7 pounds. 36 years of age. Male. With inflammation in both ankles and highly aggravated."

"Very close, but not perfect."

"Your Honor, objection! How can counsel for the defense prove this? He's sprouting rhetoric to taint the jury."

"Mr. James can you prove this?"

MLJ smiled like he wanted the question asked, "Your Honor, I have another email that will prove it." He then handed Dr. Escant his cell to download the information. MLJ narrated as the jury watched Dr. Escant's machine's analyzation continuingly changing as the figure disrobed in the public restroom. Removing the gloves, revealing it was a white person, then the jacket, the tie, the cuff links, the shirt, which was covering a short-sleeved bullet proof body armor.

"You're right on the height and the weight, adding the body armor ..." On the screen; the masked figure kicked off the shoes and unfastened the belt and pants, which fell to the floor, revealing the body armor stopped at the figure's knees. The scraps securing the body armor were on the sides. Once released the figure had to lift the body armor over her head. The jury and the people in the courtroom saw the sexy body of a white female in a matching set of silk underwear, hurrying into the shall. The woman removed the mask and shook out her long blond hair before closing the door to the stall. "... And the irritation was right. But as we all can see my wife is not a man. Stand up baby. Yeeah."

She stood and turned a circle.

Jurroda stood shouting, "Your Honor, he tricked. ..."

"A trick!"

"Your Honor he manipulated the ..."

"Your Honor these items worn in the demonstration are identical to the detail of the items taking off of the dead bank robber. I didn't create an error. The machine made an error. Dr. Escant was any of the information analyzed differently than the demonstration performed with the image of Mr. Jurroda?"

"No."

"Did you do anything different to formulate the machine's results?"

"No."

"Dr. Escant, is there a chance the masked figures in the surveillance video of the banks getting robbed, females disguised as men?" He regrettably nodded. "I need a verbal answer please?"

"Yes.

"No farther questions."

"We will adjourn for a lunch break, and resume at 1:30 PM."

CHAPTER 35

PRINCE

I respect the police, the law of the land, and yes, I'd called my self-policing my hood; but the modification of the rules changed, just like the judicial decree shows the law changes when circumstances change. I heard my name being called by the DA. I wanted to avoid being involved with the circus act.

The bailiff peeped out the court room into the hallway where I was sitting. "Prince Battle."

I entered the packed courtroom. Most of their eyes were suck on my face. They couldn't believe I was taking the stand. The ones who had sense, read my sweat shirt, then started clapping. I had on a stop snitching sweatshirt.

The DA was gritting on me as I was being sworn to an oath of truth.

Mr. Prince Battle, you are under oath. Have your home been burglarized and vandalized?"

"Yes."

"Have attempts been made to end your life along with your brothers and sisters' lives?"

"Yes."

"Do you know who is responsible for these violent acts?"

"Yes."

"Are they present in this room?"

"Yes."

"Remember you are under oath. Will you point them out?" He was testing my integrity.

I weighed the situation and was determined not to allow myself to fall victim to pressure, "You and special agent Sader. You two have made it seem as if I've been caught doing something illegal, and is now corroborating to free myself, by taking part in your scheme. Something I have no knowledge of!"

"The crowd erupted with, "Tell they muthafuckin' asses P!"

The judge brought his courtroom to order, "Another outburst like that, and I will clear the room!"

Jurroda continued with his questions, "Do you have knowledge of the defendants?"

"Yes."

"How do you know them?"

"We study the science of religion at the same hall."

"Do you work for Mr. Cuda Bay?"

"No."

"You're under oath."

The more I stood by my code of ethics, my foundation became stronger and it became increasingly easier to follow my code no matter what.

"I know I am. Are you under oath?"

"Do you work for Mr. Cuda Bay?"

"No!"

"Is Mr. Cuda Bay one of your sponsors?"

"No! My PR actually bought a percentage of Beckon's for me."

Jurroda lost his composure. "Has either of the defendants given you dye money from the bank robberies?"

"No—ooo! Your Honor I was subpoenaed here. I'm not under indictment! But the DA's questions are implying I've conspired."

"Your Honor, Mr. Battle is committing perjury."

"Mr. Jurroda! If you have proof of that, why is Mr. Battle a witness instead of a defendant?"

"Your Honor, Mr. Battle and Mr. Bay and the others are highly sophisticated, cautious criminals. Evidence is still being sought to bring Mr. Battle to justice."

"Your Honor! The DA has threatened me with a hundred years, assigned a social worker who has been attempting to put my brothers and sisters into foster homes, if I refused to help. Again, I know nothing of any bank robberies or dye money! But the DA is making good of his threat, by assassinating my character. I am a professional athlete, like Tiger Woods and Kobe Bryant. My endorsements could more than double the income from sporting events. The DA's allegations are deliberate and unlawful!"

"Mr. Jurroda! Do you have any farther questions for Mr. Battle?"

"No, your Honor."

"Mr. James, do you wish to cross examine?"

"No, your Honor."

CHAPTER 36
PRECIOUS

The signs had been there, but I was overlooking them. I'd taken them as my own good fortune. My confidence was in me. I viewed the situation as the outside forces were trying me, missing the fact that it was outside forces in my corner.

I was recouping, the school was understanding, thinking my recurring headaches were due to being shot in the head, so I was allowed to complete my school assignments at home. My bruises and swelling had almost disappeared, but my body hadn't fully recovered from the beatings. I was about 70 percent of myself after being shot.

It was Saturday morning. I was resting when the phone awakened me. It was Prince's voice, excitedly speaking in a whisper. "The police is here with a search warrant, looking for you. The warrant also has Shey's addresses listed. They could be on their way. ... Hell naw I'm not getting off of my phone! This warrant gives you permission to search for her here. Search, then get out! ... None of your business!"

Prince hadn't called because he wanted anything in return, he did it because he was my brother and he loved me, and that is what family supposed to do.

I hung up, scrambling. I'd replaced all the den furniture and had wall—papered the walls, but I still had the majority of the cash and all 20 kilos of heroine. I couldn't deposit all of the cash, so I'd been making small deposits, justifying them through the promotional business. I'd told Prince I'd thrown out the kilos, but I was planning on selling them; even if I dumped them at 50 grand, a million dollar was too much for me to throw away.

Guns were hidden all around the place. I packed everything I could find into the SUV; a backpack with at least two million dollars cash, a duffle bag of guns and the bag with the kilos. As I drove off the swat team arrived. They didn't recognize the vehicle as I passed.

Two blocks down I saw a thick flow of people; males, females, youngsters from the age of 12 to 33, with book bags, backpacks, hand bags and duffle bags. The closer I got I realized the people were entering the parking lot of First Methodist A&E. Inside the gated parking lot I could see a huge furnish with tables assembled in front of it. There were at least five different lines of people. A huge banner read; Redemption Day; Come unto the Lord, for he is our salvation. I didn't want to do it, but I couldn't risk getting a life sentence. Reasoning won out. I pulled into the first available parking space on the street. I struggled with the three bags. I could see more police cars ahead and some headed down the block away from the townhouse.

At the tables in front of the furnish, the ministers were praying with each person, making the line move at a snail's pace.

A police patrol unit had stopped to the rear of my Land Rover. I presumed, running a license plate check. It was still two people in front of me. The minister finished his prayer as I saw the police get out of their car, then started to inspect the SUV closer. The minister knew the man in front of me, reminiscing before beginning to pray.

More police had arrived and were scanning and stopping females. The minister finished his prayer, then opened the bags of guns before putting them in the incendiary. The police were in the parking lot when the minister was about to pray for me.

"Please don't pray. This is for you. You can do with it whatever you want. Just hurry and put these in the furnish. Please?" I handed the minister the backpack of cash. He hadn't said yes or no, but his eyes were saying no until he unzipped the backpack and saw the cash. He quickly put it under the table, then placed the other bags into the furnish as the officers stepped beside me.

"Excuse me Miss. Are you Precious Battle?"

I was still staring at the minister as he turned toward me with a smile.

"Yes I am."

The minister spoke before the officer, "Redemption is your's young sister. Your slate is wiped clean."

"Ms. Battle will you come with me?"

"What is this pertaining too?"

"You're wanted for questioning."

Free from the consequences of sin, the price had been paid. I had atoned. My burden had been lifted and I had no worries concerning myself. I was taken to the precinct and interrogated by the agent that was with Black at the bookstore.

"... I saw you in the bookstore. Explain that?"

"I frequent that bookstore. If you saw me. I guarantee I purchased a book."

"Bitch you think you're smart!"

"Bitch? You're a bitch! Bitch ass nigga! Shey wasn't a dope dealer, he was a promoter!"

"Your boyfriend was a dope dealer! And I have witnesses to testify to it.

"If he was, I didn't know about it."

"You took over his business."

"His promotion business."

"I know you killed Dora and Black."

"What makes you so certain?"

"They both dealt with Shey, then continued dealing with you, his girlfriend."

"Get them on the stand to testify to that, with your bad ass! Stupid muthafucka! Since you think Shey was a dope dealer, what makes you think he wasn't the stereotypical dope dealer with several girlfriends? Huh? One of his other girlfriends that knew the person you're claiming to be Shey, could've taken over that business?"

He drew back to hit me, but his partner grabbed him. A knock at the door to the room. Another officer escorted a tall distinguished white woman into the room. I'd seen her on CNN several times, defending high profiled celebrities and powerful CEO's.

Her entry sucked the air out of the room, made the agents pay attention, then cut off the officer. This is Mrs. ..."

"There's no need for introductions. Ms. Battle is my client. If she's not being charged, this conversation is over. Ms. Battle come with me." Beautiful and in control.

The agent shot his last words. "There's no statute of limitation on murder. Eventually someone always tells. Remember that Ms. Battle."

My brothers and sister along with Campbell met us as we exited the building.

My new best friend, my attorney Mrs. O'Connor hugged Campbell. "How's my god daughter?"

"Fine. Thanks for coming."

"Your father will be charged." She then suspiciously smiled at the closeness of Prince and Campbell, until Campbell spoke.

"Aunt Megan, this is Prince Battle, my boyfriend. This is his sister Phoenix and his brothers Pharaoh and Phihiem. Precious is his sister too."

 "I can pay my own bills. You don't have to charge her father."

A look of approval, "Nice to meet you all. Prince, she's a future partner of my law firm, remember that. Precious, if any new details arise, I'll contact you." Then confidently strolled to her big body Benz,

I wasn't concerned with the agent's threat, because everyone that could connect me to any crime was dead.

CHAPTER 37

CUDA BAY

What weight is to be given to each point of evidence? MLJ had submitted the affidavits of the members of the study hall and the employees that had attended my lecture on the dates of the bank robberies, as their direct testimony, establishing our alibies; 150 witnesses, which Jurroda used to drag out the cross examinations for four days,

"Are you being paid for your testimony?"

"No."

"Are you being paid for a day's work?"

"Yes."

"What time does your shift normally begins and ends?"

"6:30 AM until 4:30 PM."

"Are you at work now?"

"No."

"But you are being paid?"

"Yes."

"For what? You're not at work."

"I'm getting a paid leave."

"You're getting a paid leave, to come to court?"

"Objection your Honor!" MLJ saw the destination of the questions.

"The witness may answer the question."

"Yes."

"Who is paying you?"

"The company I work for."

"Who signs your paycheck?"

"Mr. Cuda Bay."

"So, Mr. Cuda Bay is paying you while you come to do what?"

"I don't understand the question."

Jurroda directed a smirk at MLJ before clarifying the question.

"What are you doing here?"

"I'm testifying."

"So, Mr. Cuda Bay is paying you while you come to court to testify?"

"Yes, but I'm telling the truth! They were at the study hall and the meeting in the parking lot!"

"Was Robert Murry at the meetings Mr. Cuda Bay held?"

"I don't recognize that name."

Jurroda went back to his desk and retrieved an eight by eleven size picture of a well-groomed Black man. This is Robert Murry. He was a member of the study hall, and a close associate of Mr. Cuda Bay and the other defendants. Do you recognize him?"

"Yes, I do."

"Was he present at the meeting Mr. Cuda Bay held on the date of September 29?"

"Yes."

"How do you know Mr. Murry?"

"He's a staff member at the factory and an usher at the study hall."

"At the meeting on September 29, what was Mr. Murry doing?"

"Standing post the entire speech!"

"Are you sure; from the beginning to the end?"

"Yes!"

"Are the defendants, ushers along with Mr. Murry?"

"Yes!"

"Were the defendants; ushers at the meeting on September 29?"

"Yes!"

"Mr. Murry was killed in a shootout with law enforcement, that also claimed the lives of two law officers. Are you certain, you saw the defendants present at the meeting held on September 29?"

To the best of my knowledge. ... As best as I can remember. ... I don't remember them leaving."

Jurroda did a good job casting doubt on the honesty of the witnesses' testimonies and had painted the picture that I had bought the witnesses.

Jurroda and MLJ, each summarized the evidence and argued their points, in an attempt to win the jury to their version of the case.

"The government has proven the connection, the knowledge, the personnel. ... The government is asking that the totality of the evidence presented against the defendants be examined as a whole. Their relationship to the deceased Mr. Robert Murry, their violent and sinister background, the manipulative diabolical nature of the leader of the defendants, and their separatist's attitude, birthing homegrown terrorists. This group of calculating, mundane criminals have no regard for the law. They are only motivated by their desires, their greed. Nothing else is important to them. Not the lives of the two policemen, not the life of the security guard of the bank. Not the life of their comrade, that they viciously killed instead of leaving him to be taken to a hospital. They will do anything to avoid imprisonment. We, you can't allow these predators to roam free within our society."

Jurroda sat and MLJ stood and approached the jury. "Homegrown terrorists? An unjustified fear tactic to shape your decisions. Because the government has failed to prove any connection between the crimes and my clients. My clients' past ill-advised decisions have been answered and redeemed. My clients are the prime example of rehabilitation and should be admired for establishing a company that employs 345 citizens of all genders, races and religions. Where is the separatist attitude? Mr. Murry was one out of the 180 ex-felons employed by Mr. Cuda Bay's company. In the last eight years there have been 35 of Mr. Cuda Bay's employees violated or arrested under new charges. Other bank robbers, drug dealers, car thieves, murders, and the list goes on. Must he and other employees be held accountable for someone else's actions? Knowing someone doesn't make you an accomplice. I'm not asking you to decide if there was a connection between Mr. Murry and my clients. I'm telling you; if you can beyond a shadow of a doubt say the DA has proven my clients have committed the bank robberies and murders, vote guilty. If you have doubt that my clients are guilty, you must vote to acquit."

The judge instructed the jury as to the points of law that governed the case. Everything was placed in the jury's hands as they adjourned to decide our fate in secret.

.....

MLJ had advised us, deliberation could be as quick as 20 minutes or days. He'd done a great job, but what a jury or person will accept is unpredictable, even when you've guided them to the truth.

CB2 was holding mine and his mother's hands as we walked to a nearby deli. There I sat watching my wife and son, seeing her features in him, seeing the innocence within him; the courage of not being afraid to stand up in the chair. I wanted to be there to spread and encourage his courage, so he would be confident in all aspects of life.

The few gray strings of hair and the one or two fine wrinkles in the corner of my wife's eyes, I wanted to be beside her, reminding her how much more beautiful she was becoming.

"Daddy are you sad?"

"Why do you ask that?"

"Because you're so quiet."

"I'm just enjoying being with you and mommy." My cell rang, "Yes. ... We're on our way. ... They're returning."

I didn't know if to hurry or prolong the walk. Ra and the others were arriving as we entered the court building.

"What do you think?"

The judge called the court to order. The courtroom had less than 20 people, including everyone involved in the case. It was as if every heart had stopped beating, even the central air knew to stop humming.

Complete attention was given to the foreman of the jury as she stood. Her eyes locked on the small strip of paper, only seeing the words to be pronounced as justice.

"The jury fines the defendants 'not' guilty of all accounts."

My heart lifted, and my tears fell.

The DA and Agent Sader's expressions were of revenge; one day we'll get you.

CHAPTER 38

PRINCE

Exposure is necessary, but often new experiences are scary.

Los Angeles, California, where the top 48 boxers in the world were gathered with every major news cast, columnist, blogger, sports mag and freelance writer and reporter, for the West Coast Brackets; 24 slots to be drawn, 12 fights the first round.

Fighters were being interviewed, all arrogant, cocky and dressed to the nine. I along with my brothers and sisters were doing like our mother told us, whenever we went somewhere new to us; act like you have been there before and expect to do well. But we were all excitedly star struck and Nubs saw it.

"It's the same old shit we've dealt wit for years. Just now money is involved. Ain't none of them fit to carry your jockstrap. Remember that."

"That's nasty! Who wants to carry your jockstrap?" Phoenix threw punches at my midsection, then boobed and weaved as I bounced around her, punching over her head. The cameras instantly started flashing and the reporters smiling.

"Prince! Prince! How does it feel to be the dark horse of the tournament?"

I had to pick up Phoenix as the crowd got closer. "It's nice to know I have some supporters, and I plan on making them proud."

"He's the modest one in our family. I'm not. It's obvious the analyses are blind or in the wrong field, for not picking my brother as the favorite. You can bet your house on him, if you want to get rich." Precious, smiled for her second of fame until Phoenix stole it.

"Because none of these bums are fit to carry my brother's jockstrap!"

I covered her mouth and that brought more smiles to the faces of the crowd. Everything settled down once the boxing commissioner started selecting names; mine was the seventh drawn. My opponent was a 33-year-old former heavy weight champion. The reporters noticed my crew leaving and rushed us.

"Are you going to train in LA?"

"No. We all have school Monday. ..."

"And we've got to tell mom about who Prince is fighting. And how beautiful it is out here, so she can get better and come see for herself."

The crowd became gushy over Phoenix's statement, "Is your mother's health improving?"

"She's a fighter."

"How are you going to train for the Englishman?"

"He's a skilled and powerful fighter. I've been impressed with him since I was eight years old. So, I'm very familiar with his moves and his style of boxing. I'm sorry, that's all the time we have for questions or we'll miss our plane."

.....

At the hospital, the sight of our mother's eyes, glassy and sunken in, the tubes in her mouth and nose, the noise of the weak beat on the heart monitor, the oxygen machine, pumping air into her lungs, the weakness of my mother's grip, the smell of the room; something dying or dead - all of it depleted whatever joy we were feeling.

A minister and my mother's new specialist from Britain, Dr. Jacob, a Black woman entered the room. Phoenix immediately grabbed our mother's other hand.

"Prince is fighting the Englishman. Prince is getting four point five million dollars, plus some more money from pay-per view. So, when you get a little better, he's going to buy us a house on the bench. He promised, Mama. ... You'll like LA. They say it never rains and it doesn't get cold there." It wasn't a prayer, but more of a plea, begging, giving a purpose, letting our mother know we had faith in her.

"Mr. Battle can we have a moment with you, in the hallway, please?"

Once the door closed behind us Dr. Jacob began, "Mr. Battle, I didn't want to discuss your mother's condition in front of the children. Her health has started to rapidly deteriorate. I can't give an estimation of how much longer before her body totally shuts down. We understand what your family is going through. I asked the minister here so you two could discuss arrangements for your brothers and sister to be placed at the same foster home." Her voice was caring, her eyes showed sympathy and her words had been compassionate, so the situation remained calm, but painful.

You tell the truth to your doctor, your priest and your lawyer because these people matter at the end. "Thank you for your consideration and delicacy, but my mother is still fighting."

"Son, some things are harder to face, but we have to face them." The priest was an end-of-life specialist.

"Reverend I know, believe me I know. But my family being separated isn't an option. I turn 18 in June. My mother will fight to see me take custody of my sister and brothers. Excuse me, it's our family day."

We decided to go to the movies to lift our spirits. Campbell noticed the stares from the sisters while we stood in line. The people started recognizing me, then began to ask for autographs. Campbell stepped aside with Precious, "Maybe this wasn't such a good idea."

"Get used to it. He's a celebrity now."

"But what if I'm hurting his marketability?"

"Men, mostly men watch boxing. And when they see your face and body next to him, they're envious."

"Maybe, but what about the sisters?"

"Well, just keep going to the tanning booth, and when they take pictures of you two, make sure you give them an ass shot. That

way it's hard to tell if you're cut or not. ...
Stop trippin'. What do you care what a
hater thinks? You've got him!"

Campbell was becoming self-conscious,
but she loved the public affection of me
pulling her close when the movie became
scary, and when I drank the last of her
soda.

Later that night Campbell decided to come
in for a second instead of just dropping us
off. Phoenix was sound asleep, so I had to
carry her. Campbell held open the door to
Phoenix's room for me.

"My mom and step father won't be home
until in the morning."

"I'm starting a major routine tomorrow.
Tonight is the last time for us to be
together until we win the tournament. ...
It's a big, big ole bed right down the hall."

"Precious room is next to it!"

"You'll just have to hold it in." I bear
hugged her.

She pretended not to like it, then gave in kissing me, "Me hold it in? You mean you! C'mon."

"We'll see who ..."

CHAPTER 39

PRINCE

Cold enough that the moisture from your breath froze on your lips and crystallized on your nose hairs. So cold your lungs strung from inhaling. I didn't feel it long. I'd dressed the part; five layers of clothing, but it was running that numbed all the burdens of the world, freed me as I ran the city before the sun was up. Nubs trailed behind me in the van. The fight was both our futures.

While I ran my suicide sprints on the stairs of the art museum, Nubs slept in the van. But on the way back to my home, he set the pace with the speed of the van, making me sprint the last four blocks to the house.

My new diet took up half of the kitchen table, plus I ate energy bars throughout the day, disturbing the lectures in my classes.

In gym class the football coaches spotted me on the bench press and were amazed that I hit 405 pounds 15 times.

A part of my new routine was jogging to the hospital after school, to build more endurance. Precious, Campbell and Phoenix were in my mother's room when I arrived at the hospital. The room had been rearranged with the bed facing the window. The sun shined directly on my mother. The scent of the flowers filled the room.

"I told them you would be here. But they wouldn't listen to me." Phoenix greeted me with a hug.

"We thought you weren't coming since your new routine."

"Stop it. This is my mother too. He doesn't have a monopoly on her. You don't have to apologize for being here." Precious pushed me back, as I bumped her out of the way, then pulled a chair next to my mother's bed.

"I like the room better this way."

"Mom does too. Her heart rate has increased." Precious was smirking at me while Campbell sat on the arm of the chair close to me.

"Mama likes the flowers and the sun." Before Phoenix could add more Precious took her by the hand.

"You're going shopping and to get your nails done with us. C'mon Campbell."

"Where are Pharaoh and Phihiem?"

"At the gym, where I need to be." Phoenix pulled away, then stood her ground, but Precious grabbed her hand again.

"You're not a boy. You're hanging with the girls today."

"I'm their coach!"

.....

I was in the middle of sparring at the gym when Mrs. Cuda Bay entered with Precious. Everyone recognized her and her confident stride, strutting toward the ring. My opponent lost focus and I dropped him.

I felt myself gritting at Mrs. Bay, then at Precious, for bringing that woman around me.

Precious read my grimace. "You said it; you all are partners. ... Just listen to her."

Nubs didn't say a word, he just started taking the tape off my gloves, then nodded to his office. Mrs. Bay followed me.

"I'm in the middle of training. Please make this brief?"

"Let me say thank you for your testimony."

"There's no need to thank me. I only stated the truth." I didn't know if she was friend or foe, wearing a wire or what.

"Fine. You're in a position to help the company and the community, plus yourself, by continuing to wear and endorse the company. ... I have had a staff with the help of Precious, put together an attire to blossom your image while showcasing the company."

"That's fine. Have them delivered to my home by Thursday."

.....

The hype of the fights had monopolized the television and radio. The press conferences and weigh-ins with the mind games boosted the media circus over the top. The time came for the Englishman and me to do our Q&A.

"... Well, I thought he had a promising career ahead of him, but that was when I thought he was headed to the Olympics. But that career is going to be short-lived since he had the misfortune of being selected to fight me."

"So, do you respect his boxing talent?"

"I admire his courage and determination to face the responsibilities of being the man of his family, but, he's a child stepping into a man's world when he enters the ring."

I listened, absorbing the insults, smiling, smirking almost laughing the more insulting he became.

"Prince, do you have anything to say to that?"

"I agree with all but two percent of what the Englishman has said; when a child meets the responsibilities of a man, that child is no longer a child, but, is a man!"

"Prince? Prince? What about the short-lived comment?"

"I look forward to the challenge."

"Englishman? Is it going to be a gentlemen's fight?"

"With one man? More of a flogging." He got a good laugh out of the crowd.

I laughed also and added, "Again I agree, but this time a hundred percent. Since I've been taught to respect my elders, I'm going to answer the rest of the questions in the ring. A flogging? That's the same as an old fashion butt whupping?" Asking my own question as I left the stage, grinning at the reporters and into the cameras.

A body bag was set up, when I passed it, I punched it with a left hook to release my anger. The crowd saw the dust fall from the ceiling, from the bolts loosing from the force of the pressure behind my punch.

Saturday evening, fight night.

The who's who, stars of Hollywood, world-wide royalty, government officials, celebrities from every avenue of entertainment were arriving at the MGM.

Mr. Bosco, the Hammer and Campbell and Precious were seated at ring side, watching a brutal, compelling show of force by C-Loc, a tatted gang member, that had found the art of boxing in state prison while during a manslaughter bid. He was inflicting his will on a huge Asian. The ref had to stop the fight by pulling C-Loc from behind. The crowd panicked once the Asian fell face forward to the mat. C—Loc turned toward the Hammer, mean mugging him.

I was being taped up in the dressing room by Nubs, while watching the fights by pay-per-view with Phoenix, Pharaoh and Phihiem. Warm was an understatement. My anticipation had me jacked to hear the bell.

"This bum called you a boy! A boy, I had my ear buds in blasting rap, but I could read Nubs' lips.

A knock came from the door, a head peeped in, "... It's time!"

A kiss to Phoenix's cheek, two hard pounds to Pharaoh and Phihiem. They were just as hyped as I was; it was our future.

The Englishman's name was announced first. The crowd cheered and paid respect but erupted when sinister beats and hardcore conscious lyrics echoed throughout the arena as my name rang out. I had dreamed of it a million times, so the hype didn't affect me. I was poised. I shadow-boxed to the ring. Nubs held up the ropes. I pranced while throwing a fury of combinations, making my hands look like a blur.

The flash of the cameras looked like twinkling stars.

The Englishman was staring hard. The ref gave the final instructions. In my mind, the Englishman's voice was screaming, repeating, "Short-lived!"

The bell caused the mental teleportation; only the Englishman and me, warriors in space.

I brushed away the Englishman's first punch, but he stepped on my foot and caught me with a shoulder, then a quick left that dropped me on my ass. I wasn't hurt. I was mad because he was trying to toy with me.

Nubs voice was thunderous, "Take the eight! Take the eight! Now get him!"

Like two unleashed pits, we clashed in the middle of the ring. It was as if I knew every punch the Englishman was going to throw before it was thrown. I side stepped, bobbed, ducked but instead of countering with head shots or rib shots. I landed solid, powerful, jarring shot between the shoulder and collarbone of the Englishman. If he tried to throw a righthanded punch, I targeted his right shoulder and collarbone, making him stumble backwards. The surprise and pain registered on the Englishman's face. He knew I was coming in for the kill. I saw the fear in his eyes. The pressure from my punches were causing hairline fractures, then the Englishman's bones snapped, and his shoulder jumped out of place. His high pitch scream made me pull back from delivering a head shot. His arm was dangling uncontrollably at his side. The ref quickly stepped in, stopping the fight.

"Winner by technical knockout, in the first round, Prince!"

The reporters shot questions at me as I was on my way to the locker room. I couldn't stop smiling, for I knew, financially things had changed forever for my family.

"... He was correct. It was short-lived."

.....

I had a sense of gratitude for what was going right for me and my family. I literally felt the pressure lifting. The concern surrounding my family was great. Many influential people sent their financial adviser and we listened to them all, but the overall decision was mine to diversify my investments between CD's and trust funds for my family.

Once I zeroed my mother's hospital bill, the hospital administrator's attitude turned into that of my best friend. We had been told; with money people become different, brand new, but it wasn't me or my family changing; what was actually changing was the way people treated us. Everyone was nicer, kinder, more considerate, which was highly appreciated.

Nubs didn't give a damn about the fame or the massive crowds that gathered watching my morning runs, filming me sprinting the steps. Nubs pushed me harder on my drills, in the film room, pointing out my opponents' strengths and weaknesses, then drilling me in the ring on what to watch for. "You want excellence! Get this little shit right! It's being the best at the basic shit is what makes you great!"

Intensive and repetitive, continual work on my fundamentals; for what seemed like hours – Nubs then rotated in and out, three different sparring partners, each with particular skills sets of that of my opponent.

The intensity of the high energy level of training was the feeling I would have after a fight. I would be so aroused it was hard to study at the hospital with Campbell and with being in the present of my mother's watchful eyes. Campbell could tell. She would push my hand away or bite at my hand when I tried to play with her earlobes, her soft spot.

On the elevator, it was hard for her to resist. "You're training! Don't start something you can't finish!" Then she ran once the doors opened.

.....

Even with my new found fame my teachers treated me no differently than other students, not cutting me any slack on the tests, taking points off my essay answers for incorrect punctuation, bringing my grade down to a B from an A.

CHAPTER 40

PRINCE

Instead of things becoming more tranquil, everything became a challenge. The flights to Vegas had become more hectic, women flirting with me at the airports, on the plane people constantly awakening me, asking for autographs and selfies. I stayed polite and accommodated them, but I was pissed. I hated being awakened out a good sleep, "Make sure we get first class next time, so I can get some rest."

As soon as we entered the Vegas airport, the cameras started flashing and the fans rushed me. I had to pick up Phoenix.

"We're already late for the press conference, so only two questions."

"Will it be another first round knockout?"

Before I could speak, Phoenix answered, "The bum won't last half a round with my brother!" She'd repeated what Nubs had been drilling at me.

"Looks like my conscience has spoken."

"Is the female you were hugging at the movies your girlfriend?"

"She's my sweetie."

"Is her name Campbell Bosco?"

"I said two questions. We have to go."

.....

My opponent was another ex-champ, in his early 30's, someone I'd idolized growing up. The questions were directed toward him.

"... You guys have made people fall in love with him. I'm not the evil one. I read the papers, the blogs. His story is heartfelt, and he's an admirable brother. But I, I can't let him stand in my way of regaining my belt. Once he gets into that ring all that cute mama's boy stuff and all of his personal problems don't concern me. And I'm not taking him light. I'm going to destroy him, and it won't be personal."

I only smiled, because he was talking as if I wasn't there. He hadn't even looked at me, so I smiled at him, as the press took pictures; patiently awaiting my reply. I then smiled at Phoenix, my brothers and finally Precious, they were my real motivation.

Phoenix leaned a little forward to get a better look at the fighter. "Poor baby. I hope the Lord have mercy on you, because my brother won't. You're not going to last a minute and a half. Poor baby."

Laughter erupted from everyone there. It was the perfect time to leave.

.....

The bell, Blackness. Two warriors. The clock was ticking in my head. Attack mode. Attack mode. He threw a head shot that was close, but he'd left his body open for my fury of body blows. I ducked his wild hook and countered with another none stop fury of body blows, which drove him to the ropes, then to the corner. He tried to push me off but exposed himself more. My blows cracked ribs on both of his sides.

.....

Phoenix, Pharaoh and Phihiem were in the locker room with a stop watch, counting down from 10, 9, 8, 7, watching and screaming, "NOW!" at the television as I threw a three-piece head shot, connecting with each bomb. My opponent's eyes rolled back to the whites. He was unconscious, but the ropes were holding him up. One minute and twenty-six seconds. My brothers and sister were screaming and hugging each other watching as I stood in the middle of the ring.

.....

I was on super model status while the other two remaining boxers; a big German: Hitler and C-Loc, both worn shades to cover their bruises. The reporters were more interested in me, "Where's the gang?"

"They left out on the red-eye last night. It's our family day."

Mr. Bosco and the boxing commissioner entered the conference room. Mr. Bosco played the background while the commissioner walked on the stage.

"The rules on who gets the bye are simple. There will be a coin toss."

Three referees came out with a coin and delivered it to a boxer. "... You each have a Kennedy fifty cent piece? ... The rules are; the odd man on the flipping of the coins gets the bye. The boxers' coin that land on the same sides will meet each other in the ring in three weeks. Boxers flip your coin and allow it to land on the floor."

The coins were tossed. The referees called out which side each boxer's coin had landed, so the audience and the commissioner would know.

"Heads! For Schawk."

"Heads! For Edgefield."

"Tails! For Battle."

"Schawk and Curry Edgefield will meet in the semi championship bout for the western brackets. The winner of the match will face Prince Battle for the western championship bout. Thank you for coming out."

The commissioner and Mr. Bosco left the room, but the crowd of reporters and camera crews blocked my way.

"Is this a dream come true to be in the championship bout?"

"When I win the heavy weight championship of the world, then it will be a dream come true."

"What are you going to do while you wait?"

"Prepare for my final examines. My flight leaves in an hour and 20 minutes."

CHAPTER 41

PRINCE

There's no proof that love, care and belief of others will make a person well. But it surely does no harm to know that you have loved ones displaying their affection for you.

Campbell was at the hospital with my family when I arrived. The first snow of winter had started outside the window. It was as if every flake that landed on the window caught my mother's attention. She was still thin, but some of her color had returned along with the strength in her grip.

Precious kept our mother's hands and feet well-manicured.

Phoenix was reading to our mother.

My brothers sat in the corner, silently watching our mother.

I was uncertain how my brothers were feeling. "You two want to walk with me to get a soda? Get your coats."

Phoenix paused midsentence. "Where are you all going?"

"Just stay here with the girls."

"I wanted to come too." Campbell was stepping toward us.

"This is a man thing." I gave her a wink and a smile before I left with my brothers.

It was cold outside, but everything was clear. Hundreds of stars sprinkled against the darkness. The moon was so full it looked as if it might explode.

"Prince, it's cold out here!"

"The cafeteria is inside the hospital."

"Man, it's beautiful out here."

"You don't like the cold either. Mom is the only one of us that likes the cold."

"But now I see why. Everything is so clear and still." Basically our mother would sit for hours on the stoop. She would say to clear her head. We knew she would be smoking her joints, so we didn't bother her.

"Can you see how long before she gets better?"

The truth was the basis of our communication. It gave us the reliability to depend on one another.

"I wish I could."

"We've got money now! Can't we pay somebody to make her better?" They both were pleading for something out of my control.

"Her doctor is one of the best in the world."

"We want the best!"

"We heard the doctor and preacher! We know what they told you. Dr. Jacob doesn't think mama is going to win!"

"Prince, is mama going to win?"

Tears were in everyone's eyes.

"Bruh she's fighting, just like the rest of us to keep our family together. The goal is to keep our family together. We're going to win."

"What about keeping mama alive?"

"Eventually death beats us all."

I hugged Phihiem who was unable to hold back his tears. I reached for Pharaoh who pushed away, then ran off. I started after him but slipped on an ice patch and lost my footing. I tried to brace myself for the fall, but in doing so the pressure rolled my wrist when I landed.

"Damnit!"

My scream made Pharaoh stop. They both rushed to me, concerned, "Is it broken?"

"I don't know, but it hurts." I knew it wasn't broken because I could still move my fingers.

.....

Nurse Pottier and her doctor friend were talking indirectly to me, while showing the x-ray to Pharaoh. I'd used Pharaoh's name in case it was fractured or not I was still fighting, and the boxing commissioner wouldn't have knowledge of anything.

"There's no fractures or torn ligaments. Luckily, it's just a severe sprang. I'm going to prescribe some pain pills. I recommend no physical activities for three to four weeks."

"Are you for real Doc?"

"I'm afraid so."

As nurse Pottier left the room I gave her a check for ten grand. "Thanks for your help."

"Baby you didn't have to do this but thank you."

.....

It's a lot better to initiate change while you can; than it is to try to react and adjust to change.

I was sparring at the gym. I'd switched to southpaw. Nubs jumped into the ring. "What the Sam hell are you doing! You're changing the game plan without telling me?"

"Is it a problem?"

He stared at me for a second, then grabbed my right wrist. Out of reflex from the pain I shot an overhand left that he barely stumbled out of the range of.

"If you would've hit me. I swear after I came to, I would've shot your big ass! You could've told me!"

"It's just a sprang."

Nubs allowed me to train in both styles. I was using my left for my power shots, and my right for jabs. Basically, just a shadow to set up my left because my wrist was so tender.

.....

I was hungry and exhausted when we entered our home. Precious was with a team of suits and dresses, sitting in the living room. Precious' aggressiveness kept her thinking, active, coming up with ways to help me and for the beneficial good of the family and the community.

"Before you go to the kitchen, let me introduce you to your foundation staff." All lawyers and accountants; minorities. "... Your foundation will help people with or without medical coverage, financially and will take on medical discrimination suits. So, no one else has to go through what we went through. Plus, we have a team that will beat the streets and corporate America for donations and do fundraisers. Your millions will be a gift back to the community."

Precious had learned our mother's sense of consciousness; the hidden rule of the support system in poverty; Sharing what little extra you have, because someone always had an emergency or was just in need. There's no choice. If not, the next time you're in need you would be left out in the cold. Plus, people who give help, feel better than those who receive it, and that gave meaning to my sister's life, a purpose to live.

"It sounds beautiful, lets ... Nice meeting you ladies and gentlemen. Excuse me."

Precious followed me to the kitchen. "I've done the research. I know what I'm doing."

"I believe you."

"Why are you pissed?'

"I'm not. I'm tired. But I don't like coming home to find strangers in our home."

"We're in school all day, plus we don't have an office."

"I do."

"Where?"

"Where I do business; at the gym. Not my home."

I always hated the fact my mother's store was a part of our home, people coming by all times of the day and night. I'd promised myself, my home would be for my family, and my business would be at the office.

Precious jumped at the opportunity to lease an office for the

Battle M&A foundation, next to the study hall.

.....

The sun was bright, but everyone was fighting the cold temperature. The entire community was up early Saturday morning for the grand opening.

Precious had promoted the opening and my name so that the event got national coverage.

The mayor, the city council members, local business owners, the state senators and even the Lt governor were there. But Precious had it so I was the keynote speaker. "I'm grateful to be a part of this. The Battle Medical and Assistance Foundation will help people with and without medical insurance and will take on medical discrimination law suits. This nation has supported my family during our time of need. And we are grateful to return the favor, to prevent as many people as possible from suffering or going through what we did."

The scissors were huge and fake. I pretended they were too heavy, "Help me?" My family came to assist, but we still pretended to need help, "... It's going to take all of us to accomplish this. We want everybody to help." We fanned over the mayor, the city council members, the business owners, and the Lt governor: Hands to shoulders, "I believe we can accomplish this with unity! Now!" We cut the ribbon and the cameras flashed.

The cold didn't matter. I took pictures for what seemed like hours; because more fans kept arriving wanting selfies with me.

CHAPTER 42

PRINCE

Not to fool nor falsify, but creating, maintaining and reinforcing a positive image in the mind of all.

Campbell was hesitant about travelling with my family, but I'd personally booked our first-class flights to the semi-finals. I sat between Campbell and Phoenix.

"I should've stayed in the tanning booth longer."

"You know you're trippin' for real. You're beautiful, not because you're pretty. It's the small things about you."

"Yeah, like my butt?"

"That helps, but ..." I had to hug her so she wouldn't hit me. "... It's your heart, and how sweet and caring you are. Thank you."

We were about to kiss when a line of three business men approached with camera phones, wanting selfies, starting other passengers to line up, blocking the walk way.

We thought we could blend in at Circus-Circus casino and enjoy the entertainment. We did for a while, until someone in the crowd recognized my entire family, then everyone wanted pictures and autographs.

Phoenix and the guys didn't mind watching the fight in their room, while Campbell, myself and Precious were ring side. Nubs joined us, dressed like a fly mobster. Mrs. Bay had dressed Nubs and me, but we all were beyond supermodel status. Campbell and Precious had spent the entire day picking out their dresses.

The cameras zoomed in on us, then the reporters came over. I was about to fan them away until Precious urged me to do a quick interview.

"Prince, it's rumored you fractured your wrist, and had to be x-rayed."

"It's all sorts of rumors floating around. I wouldn't listen to any rumors."

"What do you expect to see tonight?"

"A lot of power punches. These are probably two of the most powerful punchers that were in the western brackets of the tournament. Both men can knock you out with a straight jab. Boxing fans are in for a treat."

"Which one are you betting on?"

"I'm too young to gamble. They both will be a good challenge."

The lights dimmed, and the announcer started to introduce the fighters, so I took my seat. Campbell greeted me with a kiss, then wrapped her arm around mine.

The fight was a bloody slug fest, held in the center of the ring. Neither fighter giving ground. Head shots, body shots, head butts, shoulders, elbows. By the sixth round both men had cuts. Hitler's nose was broken and pouring blood, while the corner of C-Loc's, worked on his left eye, which was leaking from a gash. It was a miracle how both corners stopped the bleeding between rounds.

An overhand left slipped over Hitler's gloves and dazed him. Before he could shake off the cobb-webs C-Loc landed another haymaker, then another and another. Hitler was out on his feet, his legs refusing to go down. C-Loc continued dropping bombs, clubs.

Campbell stood screaming at the ref, "Stop it! Stop it! Stop the damn fight!"

C-Loc ignored the bell and the ref waving his arms to stop the fight, so finally the ref tackled C-Loc to stop the fight. C-Loc jumped around C-walking, celebrating his victory.

I'd seen enough. We were all walking toward the stairs when C-Loc started screaming, "Pretty ass bitch! Pretty ass bitch! Princess, you pretty ass bitch!"

I knew he was trying to get into my head, so I kept walking. But Campbell tried to pull away from me, to go back to ring side.

"Not you bitch! The bitch holding your hand! ... Yeah you. You pretty ass bitch! When you get into this ring, you're gonna become my bitch!"

I didn't say a word but Campbell, Precious and Nubs, plus several body guards grabbed me. It was a sea of blue behind C-Loc in the ring.

Nubs was money minded, "Wait, wait three weeks to knock this clown out, and we get a 15-million-dollar purse. Do it now and all we get are hospital bills. It's too many of them. Be smart."

"Yeah bitch, walk away! I'm the killer! I'm the muthafuckin' killer!"

.....

Being scared is too costly a price because you can't afford to be choosy about where the best results come from.

Reporters were camped out at the hospital. They ambushed us at the entrance. "Prince, what do you have to say about C-Loc's comments?"

"Two things. He talks too much, and I guarantee, three weeks from today he won't be able to say another word. It's family day. I, we really need to see mom. Excuse us."

"Is Campbell a part of the family?"

"As close as you can get."

My mother's doctor along with two other foreign doctors; two Asians, were examining my mother when we entered her room.

My family and my expressions were of fright and suspicion, but the doctors' expressions were of joy or excitement.

"Has our mother's condition changed?" A question I didn't want to ask.

"Can we speak to you, Mr. Battle in the hallway?"

"No. We can discuss it here in front of everyone."

Phoenix took our mother's hand into both of her hands. One of the doctors wrote down the increase in my mother's heart rate.

"Mr. Battle, with the low rate of brain activity your mother has; she's legally braindead, and her body should've shut down months ago. But to something beyond our knowledge, her internal organs continue to function at a low rate, but enough to sustain her."

"Is it a chance she could come out of the coma?"

"To be honest; she could be out of the coma. This is uncharted medical territory."

"What's next? Is she going to recover?"

"We don't know. If you allow us to experiment. ... We might be able to predict the outcome. Dr. Zocion has a new technique to remove the bullet. Dr. Lubursh will then attempt to repair the broken nerve ends by regenerating them, using stem cell injections. These techniques haven't been used on humans, but the procedures have been successful on monkeys. There is a chance for success, but the operation itself might be too stressful for your mother's body to handle."

We all were attentive, hearing every word.

"Let me get this right; You're asking me to allow you, to do something that might kill our mother, instead of saving her?"

"Mr. Battle ..."

"Dr. Jacob, we changed doctors because the last doctor wanted our mother to be a guinea pig for scientific progress. I am a strong believer in science, but I will not sacrifice our mother for its advancement."

"Mr. Battle, I'm not asking you to donate your mother's life to science. I promise you our goal during any experiment with your mother's brain will be to prolong her life and to attempt to awaken her motor skills. ... Mr. Battle if your mother is half the woman you've spoken of in your interviews. ..." She paused with a look of pleading, then continued, "... There's a chance your mother might die, but others, one day may recover from comas and regain their motor skills because of her."

"Dr. Jacob, will you all excuse us, so we can spend some time with our mother on our family day." I closed the door behind them, then noticed the stern looks on everyone's face. "... She has some nerves!"

"You're scared!"

"What?"

Precious' eyes were tight and her lips had narrowed, "You heard me! You are scared!" She was right. I was horrified of thinking about life without my mother.

"Damn right, I'm scared! I'm not you! I think before I react! So, I'm scared. I'm scared the DA is going to get someone to turn or lie on you or me! That will mean Pharaoh will be in a foster home for two years. Phihiem for four years and Phoenix would be in a foster home for seven years. So yes, I am scared if I make a decision and mom dies, things might snowball out of control!"

Precious became emotional, breaking down, "So we sit around and do nothing instead of making a decision? All we'll doing is praying mama lives until your birthday! There's a chance to save mama. Please? Please Prince?"

Campbell and Phoenix were both teary eyed. My brothers looked like they wanted to try me. They all had the face of courage, that took me pass my doubts.

"We'll take a vote. All who want to try the new techniques raise your hand." Everybody's hand went up including Campbell.

The doctors were happy to hear of our change of heart.

CHAPTER 43

PRINCE

The weight on both hands. It was the week of final examines. I'd studied but it was hard to concentrate with my mother's upcoming surgery and C-Loc's mouthing off in every interview, being blasted constantly on every sports' channel.

I was on edge. I trained five times harder and longer, it eased my mind. Nubs was concerned with my right only up to 40 percent of the power it usually had, but my left's power was as if it had increased. We had to hire more sparring partners. They weren't willing to take the pounding day in and day out.

All my teachers, but one had agreed that I could take my test on Thursday. Even the one, had agreed I could take his test with his first period class on Friday. There was only one flight leaving out on Friday, so timing was of the essence.

The test was longer than I'd expected, then there were two feet of snow on the ground, which had the traffic congested so the ride to the airport was extremely slow. To top everything, the flight had been delayed, then cancelled.

"No-ooo man!"

"Don't sweat it. I'm on it," Precious was at her best under pressure. She was already on her cell, making arrangements.

"We're going to miss weigh-in."

"No, just the press conference. ... Get the bags."

"Where are we headed?"

"To Vegas. ... To the train station, then two states over I've booked a chartered flight to Vegas."

"A private jets? ... How much is this going to cost?"

"You can afford it."

"How much?"

"$12,000 an hour."

"$72,000! for one way!"

"No. That's $14,928,000. You've saved. Now get your mind on the fight!"

.....

At the weigh-in I was jet lagged and pissed. C-Loc was spitting prison rhetoric. He outweighed me by eight pounds, but I had a four inch reach on him. He was spouting off as we faced off for the cameras. "Word on the grapevine; you snitching."

"When we get in the ring I'm going to do something nasty to you. But you can ask anyone from where I'm from, and they'll tell you I'm thorough!"

"Muthafucka! You're from Teledelphia! Ain't a damn thing thorough out of there!"

He wanted to play mind games. I had one for him; a quick two-piece, leading with my left, testing my right. It buckled him, and he staggered backwards. Two of his boys rushed toward me. I was shaking off the sting in my right wrist when Pharaoh caught one of C-Loc's guys with a right, flush on the chin; dropped him cold. The other one stopped once seeing Nubs raising an iron chair. The security guards escorted us to the limo with C-Loc screaming behind us. "That soft ass right! I'm gonna kill your muthafuckin' ass!"

In the limo, Nubs was examining my wrist.

"It's fine."

"Who're you shittin'? I've seen you punch a hole in a brick wall. That clown didn't see it coming and didn't fall."

"I know it's not a hundred percent. I'm setting him up for the left. I'm building his confidence, so it'll be easier to knock him down."

"All right now, don't be too smart for your own good."

.....

The hype had escalated around the fight. Viewership orders for pay-per-view was the highest ever.

The MGM was star studded, I was focused. The deafening cheers, the energy of the crowd, nothing fazed me. It was only me and C-Loc in our own dimension. Two straight right jabs, flush on C-Loc's mouth, stopped him from charging as I danced around in the middle of the ring. I could see the blood pooling in the corner of his lips.

"Open that mouth now! Call me a bitch now!

Before he could get the word out, I blasted him in the mouth with two more hard straight right jabs. His head snapped back and he countered with a haymaker, missing wildly.

"I'm going to get that mouth! I'm going to knock every tooth down your throat!"

The entire first round I force fed him leather. Jab and move, jab and move. The only time he touched me was to hold me. I watched him grimacing from pain as he spat out teeth with his mouth piece.

Nubs was screaming and throwing water on me. "You've had your fun! Now eat him and stop playing!"

C-Loc came out of the break, bobbing, trying to get under my reach.

I caught him with a left dead on the kisser, that put him on his ass. When he sat up, both of his lips were split, his eyes were watery, but the SOB spat out the blood and called me a, "Bitch!"

I intentionally approached so the ref would stop his count, "Get up! Get up!"

It had become more than personal. He made it up, and even through his knees were shaky the ref allowed the fight to continue. I backed off and gave him air to clear the cobwebs.

Nubs was about to have a heart attack, "Finish him! Finish him damnit!"

My first shot was a left hook to his body, then a left hook to his head that landed on his ear. His ear drum sounded like a balloon popping. He staggered into my right hook to his body, which I follow with a right hook that found its target; his left ear. He had no equilibrium. I unleashed a left hook that disfigured his face, shattering C-Loc' s jaw. My right hook to the left side of his jaw, stopped his screaming and put him to sleep.

The ref saw the blood trickling from C-Loc's ear onto the mat, then immediately signaled for the medic. The crowd cheered, and the cameras flashed. I'd beaten a man half to death and the people loved me for it. The reporters rushed me, ignoring the fact that a stretcher was taking C-Loc out of the ring.

.....

Bout number two; the following Monday morning my mother had surgery: 12 hours to remove the bullet, 13 more hours to see if it was a success. When my mother awoke, her eyes didn't recognize or study every movement. They were that of a new born, seeing objects and colors for the first time. Her grip didn't have the affection. It was more grasping because of insecurity. The doctors entered the room with smiles.

"Good evening. Great fight." Then examined and recorded my mother's vitals.

"Doc, her eyes and touch are not the same."

"If the treatments are a success, it's a strong possibility we will have to retrain your mother's brain."

"As in?"

"As in from the infant stage. There were complications. In order to inject the complete traumatized area of your mother's brain with stem cells; five more operations will be required, due to the massive damage we discovered."

Precious had surfed the web and found successful stories on the medical use of stem cell research. She'd made everyone read it to calm our worries and to strengthen our faith. "Are we facing the same risk as we did in this operation?"

"Yes, the recovery time is calculated within a seven-month period."

"We'll have mom back in seven months!"

"Be quiet Phoenix, and listen. Six brain surgeries within a seven-month period? Where is the recovery time?"

"The use of stem cell shortens the recovery period to a fifth of the normal time needed. Mr. Battle, we are under a time period. Due to the severity of damage done when the bullet entered your mother's brain: Seven months might be too long to wait. ... This is my personal cell number if you have anything to discuss."

CHAPTER 44

PRINCE

All questions have an answer, just ask enough questions. Pharaoh, Phihiem and myself were in the ring doing foot work drills to Nubs' shouting. It was almost choreographed.

"Dance! Dance!" Two steps to the right with a right hook to the body, then the head. "Freak it! Freak it!" Two steps to the left with a left hook to the body, then the head.

Over and over, then when Nubs got tired of shouting at us, he relinquished command to Phoenix; who had her own flare, "Wiggle with it! Wiggle with it! No-ooo! No, no, no! I want you to bob and weave and slide back to the dance side! Unless I say; freak that wiggle! Now back to grooving! Dance!

Dance! Wiggle with it! Wiggle with it! Now freak! Now freak that wiggle! ..." Two hours straight.

"Without work, nothing works, so do it!"

We'd hit the showers and were headed out, when I remembered the DVDs of the Last 24 fighters were in Nubs' office. Nubs was watching sports center. The commentator was interviewing John Henry, better known as the iron man, a southern brother from Birmingham, as big as the old fable. His southern draw made you think he was slow or just dumb, but he was neither.

"... With Gnon out ..." A big Russian, who'd caught his wife cheating and killed them both with his bare hands. "... do you see anyone stopping you from meeting Prince Battle?"

"Prince Battle is one of Bosco's gimmicks. Every fighter in the eastern division brackets will punish Prince. Prince Battle is a joke."

"Whoa! Be careful! The last three fighters that were disrespectful, careers got ended after they fought Prince Battle."

"He beat two has-beens, got the bye, then out boxed a brawler. Please! He had a road map. A blind man can see that. This tournament and Prince Battle are cash cows for Bosco. I beat the Hammer, and the world knows it."

"It was a pretty close fight, but he did get a knockdown."

"I slipped! Prince has a great slob story. He's marketable; doing things for the community. The world loves him. He's the great underdog, but Bosco knows he's not ready to face off with the Hammer. But when I face Prince, the ref won't be able to save him. I'm going to knock him out. Then I'm going to handle the Hammer."

"Some say Prince Battle has brought boxing back to life."

"Yeah. Folks are into boxing again, but you've got to thank Bosco, Prince's promotor."

"You seriously think Mr. Bosco is manipulating boxing?"

"I was in his stable. I learned two important things about the man; he's about his money and his family. And Prince Battle has to be considered a part of Bosco's family because he's dating Bosco's daughter."

Nubs noticed me, then turned off the television. "You're going to have your haters"

"Turn it back on. I want to hear what the analysis's say. Turn it on!"

There was a panel of three analysis's, "No comment! ... No comment! ... Well, I'm going to tell it like it is. I ain't afraid of Frank Bosco. I like the kid, but without help, he can't beat anything that comes out of the eastern brackets. No one!"

Nubs turned off the television again, "You're the underdog. You're new to the scene. They don't know what to expect from you."

"Gas up the van!"

"What for?"

"Gas up the Van! We're going to New York!"

I was deep into my feelings. A million questions. Maybe too deep. I was questioning my own abilities.

The ride was a needed cool down period, but I had to know the truth. It was Campbell's weekend to be with her father. She was surprised to see us. "Prince! Is something wrong?"

"I need to speak with your father."

She became seriously concerned. "it's ten minutes to eleven."

"I know what time it is! Is your dad here?"

"Calm down. What happened? What is this about?"

"Did you ask your father to make it easy for me to win the western division of the tournament?"

"I-I ..."

"She told me she loved you. She told me how you were fighting more outside the ring, then in it. ..." Mr. Bosco was standing at the top of the stairs in his pajamas and reading glasses.

"... Did you manipulate the tournament?"

"It's my tournament!"

"It's my name! My life you're tainting!"

"You won the fights! You did it!"

"You didn't have the right to set up the brackets so I faced the weaker opponents! I am a fighter, not a gimmick! Regardless how much love your daughter and I share, it didn't give you the right!"

"He was only trying to help."

"Help, by destroying my reputation? I don't want anyone second guessing my career."

"Son, don't allow your pride to distort the big picture."

"The only picture I see, is that you have me painted as a do-boy, being set up for the big fall."

"You made 72 million dollars in two and a half months. If you …"

"… If I don't step up, no one will ever respect me as a fighter. … Since Gnon isn't going to compete, put my name in the drawing for the eastern brackets."

"Nubs, he's your fighter! Do something now!"

"Prince, the purse for the tournament championship is 30 million, plus your percentage of pay-per-view. Then your 30 million take from the WBC title bout."

"No-ooo! Nubs, you knew about this?"

"What!" Nubs' eyes gave him away.

"30 million is the loser's take. It was in the newspaper! ... You're fired! ... Mr. Bosco, there's a clause in our contract that allows me to opt out under any unscrupulous business transaction. I will invoke it if you don't enter me into the drawing."

"I'm going to do it! But answer this; why are you doing this?"

"So there won't be any questions."

.....

The van was silent while we rode to the Ritz Hotel. Phoenix punched Nubs as we got out, "How could you? Are you just dumb or just don't believe in him?"

Our faith in one another was my family's true strength. It brought out the best in us. It was the difference between the fear of failure and the courage to try. It let us knew we weren't alone. It fortified us as a family, as a team.

I'd decided to keep Nubs on as my trainer, but it suddenly depended on his answer, if he would be dismissed all together.

"I got greedy. The short cut looked sweet. We all needed the money. Kid, you're the greatest fighter I've ever seen."

"You're not my manger any more, but you're more than welcome to stay on as my trainer. I'll get a contract drawn up when we get back to Philly."

.....

Plain and simple, so there's no interference in the message, I'd called Precious that night and updated her on my decision, and she'd taken it from there. She and Campbell arrived at the hotel the following morning with everyone's clothes.

"After the drawing, you have an interview on sports center. We're going to broadcast from back in Philly. These are the questions they're going to ask."

Campbell looked gorgeous but kept her distance until Precious pushed her to me. "Don't be a punk now! Go on over there."

......

The news hadn't broken, so everyone was surprised when my family and Campbell entered the hotel's banquet room, where the drawing was about to take place. I sat across from John 'Henry. I had to see his reaction when he heard my name. The only difference in us was, he was blue black. Our jaw structure and built were close to the same

Mr. Bosco and I made eye acknowledgement, the Hammer was too busy eyeing Precious' cleavage that her business suit revealed.

The camera zoomed in on me when my name was called and placed in the third bracket against Trinidad, a light heavy weight that had unified all the belts at that level but found it too hard to maintain the weight, so he'd moved up and put his name in the hat.

As soon as the commissioner finished, the cameras and mics were all shoved in my face, "Prince? Prince? Prince? Explain why?"

"Your fans won't understand," The only statement that registered.

"To all of those who don't understand my reasoning, watch my work."

I was mean mugging John Henry who had an understanding smirk.

"Don't be concerned with me. You better be ready for Trinidad. I'm going to be there, just make sure you're there."

The camera swung back to me, but I remained quiet, because he was right.

CHAPTER 45

PRINCE

The evaluation of the source of the message will relate to trust worthiness, credibility, reliability and ethical stance in the mind of those who receive it.

On the steps leading up to the art museum, where Precious had set up to broadcast live via satellite, my interview with sports center.

The entire city seemed to be there.

"The question is why."

"There're several whys; I represent the poor and the masses. I fear no man. No one will dishonor the legacy I'm building. I'm sick of people speculating, guessing. I'm creditable, capable, accountable and responsible, and I've got the willingness to struggle to achieve. ..." The connection got lost. The crowd loved the answer.

Precious had pulled the plug strategically, which worked; we watched on the laptop as the ESPN analyses went berserk.

"He's mad. He has a bigger purpose. He's the most dangerous fighter to face now. I wouldn't want to be Trinidad."

"I admired the kid. He has balls, big ones! But the skill level, power and experience of Trinidad will prove too much for the kid to handle."

.....

Readiness; Nubs brought in light weights to spar with me, to match Trinidad's sped. Once I adjusted to their pace; Nubs had to pay them triple to continue to spar with me.

Since the acquittal of Cuda Bay, every woman in the neighborhood had become my personal chef.

Precious kept herself busy by keeping my PR national, leaking to the media that I would be giving donations to schools needing new technology, books, more teachers and science departments. I gave one million dollars to nine schools, not including two million to Phoenix's elementary, the two million to the middle school Pharaoh and Phihiem attended and the two million to my school – in Precious and my name. The donations were all tax deductible plus the schools needed it, except my high school.

The assembles at the schools were fulfilling; I was able to use the success I'd achieved in the ring to contribute to the greater good.

Brooke passed me in the hallway but couldn't look at me.

My mother had started moving her toes and fingers. Her second surgery was scheduled for January 11th, two days after my fight with Trinidad.

CHAPTER 46

PRINCE

Unlikely, at a disadvantaged, inferior; the underdog but motivated to struggle. Atlantic City, the place of the Eastern tournament fights. The press conferences and weigh-ins were different. Still mind games, but more respectful; everyone respected the level of skill of their opponent.

The first four fights went the distance. The judges had to make tough decisions. The fifth fight was John Henry against an Australian, 'Rock', whose determination gave John Henry the blues. Fatigue became a factor in the eighth round, and John Henry's conditioning prevailed. He crumbled the Rock with crushing blows in the corner.

My fight was the main event, the stay up draw card. The critics had noted it as possibly being the best fight of the tournament as of yet, but they still had picked Trinidad to be victorious.

Trinidad didn't have any weak areas on the mat, and he was quicker than the light weights I'd trained with. Jab and move. Jab and more, then he would throw a quick combo and run. He wasn't out boxing me, but he was out scoring me. His punches were like annoying stings, but I knew later on they would feel like gunshots.

"Forget the head! Work his body! Work his goddamn body!" Nub loud roar echoed throughout the ring.

Trinidad tried a fury. His head was open, but since I'd missed so many times because of his reaction speed, I shot a hard left hook to his solar plex. The power of my punch made him stagger backwards. Before I could step forward for the kill, the bell rang and the ref jumped between us.

The confidence that had been in his eyes became glazed with doubt.

Nubs saw blood. "Be patient. Be patient. You don't have to kill'im wit' a head shot. Tenderize him. Beat his body, then sooner than later you'll be able to chop off the head!"

By the fifth round Trinidad's jab had my right eye almost swollen closed, but the results of my right and left hooks to Trinidad's solar plex had his entire chest purple.

I'd cut the ring in half, and the rounds had slowed Trinidad. I had been as coy as a panther, stalking while guiding, cornering, then pouncing. Body blows, body blows, merciless body blows. I wasn't an underdog, I was a black panther, and Trinidad was my prey. He lowered his elbows, but was still defenseless, leaving his head unprotected. My left hook snapped his head one way, then my right hook caught him and spent his limp body through the ropes, out of the ring. It was so vicious it scared the audience to silence. Nubs jumped the ropes and excitedly lifted me, and the crowd cheered.

It took four days for the swelling around my eyes to go down, but I couldn't sit around and wait. At school, I received the girls' sympathy. At the hospital, my mother's doctors were concerned if I needed pain pills. My mother's second surgery was successful. The stem cells injected into the broken nerve endings were regenerating.

"Both of your mother's lungs are up to 60 percent."

Campbell kissed me at the sound of the good news and slid a condom into my hand. It had been close to three months since we'd made love. Our passion was a spiritual journey, melting into oneness. Neither of us woke up until my alarm clock went off to start my run.

"My mom is going to kill me!"

"Your cell hasn't rung. Maybe they haven't realized you're not at home."

"My battery is dead, that's why!"

Campbell arrived late for school. "My mom took my car and grounded me for two months. I won't be able to attend your fights."

"Is that it?"

"My dad is coming to Philly this evening, to talk face-to-face."

I was in the middle of sparring when Mr. Bosco entered with two huge body guards and Campbell. They came ring side and waited until Nubs stopped the session, "Get over here! ..." Then whispered in my ear, "She's pregnant, huh?"

"I used a condom."

Mr. Bosco became impatient, "Nubs can we use your office?"

"You've got to remember they're kids."

"Can we use the damn office!"

"Go on!"

I was watching Campbell's sad eyes. She was a daddy's girl, and had let daddy down.

"Prince, son, I need to see you in the office."

I slowly trailed them into the office. As soon as the body guard closed the door, Mr. Bosco's face transformed showing his rage. "Is my daughter a groupie to you?"

"No sir."

"She must be! You've got her staying out all night. ..."

"... Daddy, he didn't make me stay out. ..."

" ... Be quiet Campbell! Before I ... My daughter has always had her own mind. ..."

"... Sir, she still does."

"Be quiet and listen! ... Campbell has dreamed her entire life about going to Yale, and from what she's told me; you're planning on attending Harvard. Your circumstances might have changed your plans, but not my child's. You two might think what you're feeling is love, but you're too young to know. My decision isn't about race or boxing, because I really like you kid, but your relationship with my daughter has become too serious. And it is distracting her from her goals. So, I can't allow you two to date any longer."

"Daddy you can't do that! I'm not a child!"

"When you finish Yale, you can do what you want. As of right now, you do what I say."

"Daddy but we love each other!"

"Do you understand me!"

Campbell's tears fell as she nodded.

"Mr. Bosco ..."

"This isn't open to debate. You have enough distractions. Concentrate on your fight, your schooling and taking care of your family, I'm going to take care of mine. Do you understand me!" He then looked at his two body guards before back to me. "I'm not making a request. Do you understand me?"

"Yes!"

CHAPTER 47

PRINCE

There's a monster in us all. My next opponent was a hairy 'Monster' from Canada. A beast who had a four-inch reach on me and outweighed me by twelve pounds. As I watched the tapes, it was obvious the creature had no flaws. He was a boxer and a brawler, smart and aggressive, and could take a punch from the best of them. He only had two losses in his career; one to the Hammer, and the other to John Henry. He'd gone the distance with both.

The Monster tried to bully me in the ring, cutting it off as if I was running. I was only feeling him out. The game plan was to meet aggression with more aggression, so when he stepped in to corner me, my two-piece chin check, backed him up. My combo would had dropped everyone else I'd fought. It only dazed him, but before I could get off again, he pushed away and cleared his cobwebs. He was stronger than anyone I'd ever fought.

I cut off the ring. He didn't like the fact I was the hunter. I stopped his charge with a two piece, which he blocked. I shot body blows, which he blocked. I mixed a body, head, body; triple blast, which he blocked. I was keeping him on defense, waiting on an opening. I was bobbing, staying under his reach, in tight when I caught a quick short right hook that made me step back. I saw him loading up with the left, so I pushed him as hard as I could before he could pull the trigger again. The force of the shove sent him to the ropes. I was still in a fog, but saw him bouncing off the ropes, so I dug in and shot a hard body blow that stopped his momentum, made him cover up and gave me time to get my senses straight.

I'd shrunk the ring to a corner, not that he was running, but I wasn't giving him breathing room. We both were slugging and covering, in tight. The hair on his chest and shoulders were like brittle pads. I was determined not to allow him to muscle his way out of the corner. Being bullied was frustrating him; he shot a low blow that made the ref step in, warning him. It allowed him separation.

Once the ref moved, instead of punching him, I shoved him. He swung wildly, barely missing. I shoved him again. I had him back in a corner, leaning on him, throwing body blows, head shots, nothing was getting in, but he was more defensive than offensive. He shot another low blow. The ref was out of position to see. Luckily it only grazed me. I retaliated with a quick right hook. I missed with the punch, but my elbow caught his chin. It rocked him, and he had to grab me, so I couldn't finish him. The bell rang.

Nubs was grinning, salivating, showering me with water while watching how frustrated the Monster's corner was.

"Just keep manhandling him, and eventually he'll cry and break.

Watch his quick hook. Lay on his right side and dig into him!"

We met in the center, both determined not to be punked. Bomb and cover, blow for blow, toe to toe. Both of our corners were screaming at us, "Get out of there!"

He headed butted me, so I caught him with a thumb in the eye. I landed a gut check that made him spit out his mouth piece. He grabbed me again, but this time he tried to slam me. We slammed each other to the mat. The ref warned both of us. Frustration had the Monster in a rage. I got on my bicycle and he willingly followed me into the corner, where I stung my trap and went on the attack, throwing everything at him in furies. Spinning him, cornering him in the corner, pushing him so he couldn't grab me. A punch slipped in that hurt him. I knew the bell was about to ring, so I was trying to finish him. The bell rang and the ref quickly stepped in, but as I was stepping back he threw a haymaker in the form of an overhand left over the ref's shoulder that landed on my jaw and sent me stumbling towards my corner. The ref deducted a point, but I was hurt, close to being knocked out.

Nubs acted as if cleaning blood out of my nose while holding my head, but he was keeping me sturdy so I wouldn't jerk and give away it was a smelling capsule he was actually putting up my nose.

"Stay away from him until you clear your head. Don't get mad, get even."

I jabbed and held, jabbed and held. By the time he'd cornered me the cobwebs were gone, but I played possum against the ropes. When he moved in for the kill, I attacked; a three piece that staggered him. I guided him across the ring dropping bombs until he bounced off the ropes, then I dug into his body, breaking his exposed ribs. The roar of the crowd drowned out his screaming moans. He lowered his guard to protect his ribs, allowing me to put him out of his misery with a quick left hook.

CHAPTER 48
PRINCE

Many know the value of opportunity and will kill for a chance. The handling of the coin toss was different, there was a Q&A session first; Media hype. John Henry, myself and Gritty: a scrappy hardnose boxer out of DC that had only been boxing for two years. We were the remaining boxers seated on stage, taking questions.

"Prince? How do you transform your wholesome loveable self, to the terror you become in the ring?"

"I've never thought of it that way. I guess I think about my life. The average poor family, how hard it is when the bottom is the ceiling we're climbing to reach. It becomes the motivation, the energy that drives me, not allowing anyone or thing to stop me.

"So it's personal when you step into the ring?"

"Is that question also for me? ... We are warriors, in a fight where there can only be one winner. It's very personal in the ring."

"John Henry, Gritty. You both have made negative comments about Prince's level of skill. Now that he has done something neither of you were able to do, do you have anything to say or retract?"

"I beat Monster."

"Yes, but Prince manhandled him, and knocked him out."

John Henry looked away from the reporters and focused on me, complete eye contact. "I said and still believe you are a gimmick of Mr. Bosco. But I was wrong about you being a joke. I think you are a force to be reckoned with." Even enemies can have respect.

"I'm standing by what I said; he's a fluke, a lucky fluke, that's trying to buy the people. I'm the people's champ. I rep for the streets!" Gritty was foolish. A talented fool.

"I'm not buying, I'm giving back to the streets!"

"I give to the streets too! The only reason I'm looked at as a thug and you're loveable and wholesome is because you're a high yellow house nigga! And I'm from the field; which is the streets! That's the only reason you've gotten the deals, and the media loves your sell out ass!"

I was in my feelings over being called a nigga. "Man if you call me a nigga again, I'm going to break your jaw."

"I knew you weren't a nigga! Where's your white girlfriend? Soul brother."

"I'm a Black man! An African American! If you had a better understanding of history, you would agree with me!"

"You're a nigga and that's the bottom line! Nigga!" Jumping up, laughing, but staying out of my reach while repeatedly saying, "Nigga! Nigga!"

I'd played into his game, but he'd showed his hand, his strategy; countering, and hit and run. Security got between us, and the commissioner hurried out once the media had been worked up. The coins landed, and John Henry couldn't believe he'd won the bye. I only nodded toward Gritty, then left the room.

The press was ridiculously interviewing people on my block, the students and teachers at my schools, the nurses at the hospital.

Precious had come up with a strategy to use the media to our advantage to create an interest and understanding of me. The objective was to convey a consistent complete favorable message, building a long-term relationship with my fans, in turn, significantly branding my recognition, "After all, we now live in a highly dynamic business environment. A global one. So, we need this global medium."

A beat the streets foundation, which promoted concerts. A simple concept. The first concert would be free to the people. Since I was paying for it, the artists were mine and Precious, and Phoenix and my brothers' favorite rappers or rap groups. All other promotions by the foundation would generate revenue to fund scholarships and community business grants. The scholarships would be based on the person's character and family's income. Creativity, capability and demand within the community were the factors examined for the grants. I paid for and choose the first two winners; Brooke, was the scholarship recipient. She was smart, caring and ambitious. All she needed was a break. She'd hurt me, but she'd been there through so much. The business grant went to a widow in my community. She'd lost her husband and both sons by the hands of the inner circle, my old crew. Her husband and sons were deserving of death, for selling death on my block - but the stress on the woman, trying to maintain the family restaurant legitimately, that legitimately employed 15 people from the community was admirable.

Precious was controlling the image the world had of me; but the giving gave me a more complete feeling from being involved in community service giving back, helping others to become winners.

CHAPTER 49

PRINCE

My mother's recovery was advancing. Her health was returning; her heart rate, lungs and the color of her skin were all close to normal.

She still hadn't moved her legs or said a word.

Dr. Jacob was changing the bandage and examining our mother while we watched.

"When will my mother be able to talk?"

Phoenix had asked, but Dr. Jacob looked at me. "If everything continues as planned, before the final surgery. Your mother's Broco and Wernicke centers were the damaged parts of her brain. They govern her verbal expressions and her comprehension. If the surgeries are successful, she will regain them, but at an infant stage."

Phoenix tried not to cry. "She's not going to remember us?"

Precious hugged Phoenix, consoling her. "At least we'll have her back. You'll, we all will be able to make new memories with her."

We all were sad, but it was encouraging news.

CHAPTER 50

PRINCE

Inching closer. The formula was working, so we stuck with it; Every fight, your best had to get better.

Gritty had natural talent but hadn't taken time to develop it. Nubs, Phoenix and I went over the footage and focused on the one fight Gritty had lost. It was to Monster. Gritty was an excellent counter boxer, but the Monster had plain over powered him.

This time Nubs brought in fly weights with hands as quick as lightning. I would throw one punch but would catch three before I could recover. By Thursday it was one to one. By Tuesday of the following week, it was two to none; we'd figured out the harder I hit, the slower the counter. But that type of energy being exerted would have me drained for the latter rounds. Nubs increased my carbs intake, to provide my body with more energy. I also spent more time on the toilet.

Since my donation, tests on Thursday instead of Fridays were not a problem. The press conference drew as much attention as a fight. The media was expecting a fight.

"... has the fact Gritty called you a house nigga, motivated you? ... Prince? Prince?"

It was hard to keep a serious look on my face, because I kept thinking of Phoenix trying to teach me how to look serious. I didn't answer. I stared hard at Gritty who was dying to spit out his comeback. He blurted out, "It's the truth! If it wasn't for his high yellow skin, he wouldn't be the favorite, at least not the media's love child."

Like any mother, the media; the reporters defended me. The Monster pushed you around the entire bout. Prince punished and toyed with the Monster. Should you be the favorite?"

"I don't fight for the critics! I do this for the hood!"

I countered with a speech Precious had written, "I'm a light complexed African American Man. I'm lucky enough to had known and loved my dad. He and my mother, and my lifelong friend and trainer; Nubs, my instructor of the science of religion, Cuda Bay, my brothers and my sisters - have all in their own way taught me to fight for what I want and need, and not to expect anyone to give me anything.

What's the use of complaining if you're not going to fix it? ... Through preparation, persistence and patience success is inevitable. So with every fight, in and outside the ring, I stand for my heritage, my nation, my family and all of mankind." I left the stage and Gritty who had no comeback.

At the weigh-in, I realized the new diet had added six pounds of muscles. Gritty was hyping himself up, talking loud to his entourage, "A yellow muthafucka ain't never beat me at shit! I'll be damned if I let a soft ass yellow muthafucka whup me!"

Gritty was eleven pounds lighter than me. He hadn't said nigga, so I only mean mugged him for the faceoff picture. Everything about me had him second guessing, trying to figure out what I was thinking.

.....

I was conscious of everything but could only hear the music blasting from my iphone while Nubs taped my gloves. I was reading Phoenix's lips. "He called you a nigga! A nigga! Mama said don't let anybody call you a nigga! Precious said, light skin Brothers are back in, anyway. You hear me Prince!" She took out my ear buds. "Whup his butt for calling you a nigga!"

I didn't wait to feel Gritty out. My first punch dropped him. He took the count until eight, then tried to dance the cobwebs out. My two piece sent him to the ropes. Power blows, "Call me a nigga! Say it! Call me a nigga! Say it!" I was teeing off on him in the corner, "... Say it! Say it! Say it!" Gritty slumped down to one knee, then fell forward.

John Henry was ring side with his wife. He had a welcoming grin, but his wife's face showed fear and horror. The ring became full of cameras and reporters, "Do you think John Henry still believes you're a gimmick?"

"If he does, he'll have his chance to prove it."

"How does it feel to be only 17 years old and only two fights from being the heavy weight champion of the world?"

"I'm focused on John Henry, one of the greatest boxers I've ever seen. Nothing else matters until I get pass him."

"Where's Campbell?"

"She's probably in her room, glued to pay—per-view."

"Why isn't she here to celebrate your victory with you?"

"I have four weeks to prepare for John Henry. Concentration and energy are a must. I love you all."

CHAPTER 51

PRINCE

Day and night, good and bad, hot and cold - they go together, inseparable. Campbell and I kept our distance at school, but it was hard, especially still sharing the same locker.

I'd realized how much I loved her. I tested the water to see if she felt the same.

"Your dad could be right. What do you think?"

She walked away mad, speechless mad, then I received a text from her in my next class. 'He's wrong! Me loving you, won't stop me from graduating from Yale.'

After a few more text messages we were back to having lunch together. Eventually we touched, then started back to holding hands and sneaking kisses in the back halls. No physical contact took place outside of school.

CHAPTER 52

PRINCE

Combined spiritual care and medical care. It matters a great deal whether a person knows they're loved. The third operation on my mother had been completed, and my mother had started rolling over, but she still hadn't made a sound. It was hard for us to leave her when she was awake; if we attempted to leave the fear of being alone would register in her eyes. Precious hired a few of my mother's best friends to sit with her through the night and until 3:30 in the evening, until Precious got there after school. It was all to make our mother as comfortable as possible.

CHAPTER 53

PRINCE

Art and science, finesse and force, mental power. Our strategy for John Henry was to confuse him. We designed attacks that looked like retreats, and attacks that were actually retreats. Nubs drilled me on being patient until the opening presented itself. He had me sparring with my hands tied together in front of me, so that I could only be defensive; bobbing, weaving, ducking and blocking shots – all to build my patience and so I could focus on openings.

At the press conference John Henry was defensive, "His performance has answered all questions. But I still believe the deck is stacked against me, and I have to knock him out in order to win. I won't get a fair shake if I leave it in the judges' hands."

"Why leave anything in anyone's hand, when you can do it yourself?"

"You have a lot to learn about life." John Henry was only 26 years old, and I didn't appreciate him talking down to me.

"What I've learned so far, is, the cause might be someone else doing; but the resolution is within me."

I don't know if he agreed or was confused, because he remained silent. The tension was expected, but overall the press conference was respectful.

The anticipation for the fight had grown. The media built the fight as the clash of the two greatest warriors of our era – but there we were, both cautious of our first move, testing the water with jabs, waiting to counter. I eventually stepped in with a fury of combinations, then bounced off, dancing. Furies, then dance. Furies, then dance. Then I mixed it up in the last 15 seconds of the round, looking for an opening while trying not to make a mistake. We were evenly matched physically, and both knew it would boil down to mental strength.

It was a calculated battle; punches thrown for later effect. Shots to elbows, shoulders, hips; all to gain any edge. By the fifth round, the 15 second mix-up, was bomb and duck. By the ninth round John Henry had become more aggressive, feeling I was ahead on the score cards. I was out punching him, but I was on my bicycle, back peddling. My jabs were on target, but I didn't have time to plant and put full force behind them, so John Henry walked through them.

John Henry threw a punch that barely missed my chin, but I tripped over my own feet and the ref called it a knock down. I jumped up explaining to no prevail. John Henry tested me by charging. I caught him with a quick left hook that landed on his chest, then followed with a fury of body shots. I had to duck his left hook, that I felt the wind from. The bell rang. Nubs and I were both tempted to change our game plan. I'd landed some hard blows and thrown more punches, but we weren't sure the judges saw it the same as us; because by design, it seemed as if I'd been running from John Henry the entire fight, when I really was waiting on and trying to create an opening to attack.

"What are you going to do?"

The trust I had in Nubs had built my confidence. I believed in my corner. "I'm going to stick with it." Except for the slip, our strategy was working. It had John Henry uncertain.

The way John Henry came out to start the tenth round, as if he was thinking he needed to land that knockout punch. My furies frustrated him as much as my retreats. His punches weren't as calculated. I could see the rage in his eyes. I lured him to the center of the ring, instead of the corner. It looked like a slug fest with both of us in close, but I was bobbing and weaving, ducking and blocking, waiting on an opening and making John Henry exert as much energy as possible. Neither of us landing that finishing blow.

The fans were on their feet the entire round, then stood with the bell for the eleventh. I enticed him back to the center of the ring. His fearlessness made him reckless, throwing bombs; hooks, overhanded haymakers, uppercuts, all missing or being partially blocked, rendering them ineffective. The crowd was amped, cheering. Nubs was screaming to abandon the plan, "Get the hell out of there!"

I saw a partial opening after his overhand right had missed wildly. My left hook was aimed at John Henry's chin, but landed on his shoulder, and left me exposed and off balance. John Henry also went for the head kill instead of the body; his first mistake: missing, virtually leaving himself in the same exposed off balanced circumstance as I was. My right hook landed hard in his lower ribs. It hurt him, but he knew my pattern body, head, body combination - so he raised his arm to block the head shot; his second mistake, because I expected he would. So I doubled up on the body. The pain of his ribs cracking made him lower his guard for protection; his final mistake; leaving his head vulnerable. I put every drop of energy I had left into my right hook to his jaw. It was as if he fell in slow motion, then bounced when he hit the mat. I couldn't believe it when he went into a push up stance. I realized I was tapped out; I had no energy left. I was over joyed when he fell to his chest. I fell to my knees and Nubs tackled me.

Pandemonium broke out, wild celebrating in the crowd, but John Henry's wife ran into the ring, crying as she checked on him.

CHAPTER 54

PRINCE

Science doesn't deal in supernatural explanations, but our brains and bodies contain an awful lot of spiritual wiring. My reception at the airport when we returned to Philly was like a parade. It was gratefully appreciated, but the audible of hearing my mother crying like a baby was a bitter sweet pill I willingly swallowed. Her progress was so significant.

Precious cried praises "Thank you God! Thank you God!"

Precious hugged the doctors, then our mother who stopped crying and snuggled next to Precious. Science had created the miracle, the answer to Precious' prayers.

"... With the speed of recovery occurring, and the strengthening of your mother's immune system, she should make a complete recovery, unless some unexpected complications arise. ..." I surprised Dr. Jacob during the middle of her statement with a hug. "... Your mother is a medical miracle that will save millions in the future."

Somehow the news of my mother's health leaked to the press. Psychologists from all over the world started calling, volunteering to try new learning techniques to speed up my mother's learning abilities. We decided not to make a decision until the surgeries were completed.

CHAPTER 55

PRINCE

School was out for spring break. Campbell's parents had given her permission to go to the Keys with the school. But instead, she was playing wifey with me. We hadn't told anyone, so Precious snapped, became overly protective when she entered my mother's bedroom and interrupted Campbell and my love-making session. I really couldn't say anything.

"You want her dad to kill you! And you must want me to kill your dad, because if he touches my brother, I promise you..."

"Precious! Precious what do you need?"

"We need to schedule a press conference. You're getting a lot of email about mom. And Mr. Bosco emailed you, reminding, you have an appointment with him in NYC in the morning."

"Email Shun and remind her I'm picking her up at 5:30. Wait until Monday to schedule the press conference, so they'll have the entire week to talk about it. Now get out!"

Shun was my lawyer and a friend of my mother's, so Precious wouldn't allow me to go to NY without her. We did our brain storming during the ride.

The Hammer, a suit and Mr. Bosco were in the conference room when we were escorted inside. The formalities were handled.

"Where's Nubs?" The Hammer was concerned about Nubs. "Where's your trainer?"

Shun took over the conversation, "My client have a few suggestions that will benefit each fighter. The fight needs to be moved to the Garden. ... An independent team to vet the judges ... and ref. The date of the fight to be scheduled on June 28, and a guaranteed rematch, win or lose within a four-month period. Everything else in the contract my client is willing to accept."

Before the suit could speak, Mr. Bosco raised a hand, silencing him. "Are you questioning my integrity?"

"The vetting is of the judges and the ref."

"Son, I like you more and more each time we talk. Add the suggestions into the contract."

.....

Monday morning after I finished my suicide sprints on the steps of the art museum, I gave my press conference. "... Before I get to the business at hand, I would like to update you on my mother's health conditions; Due to the breakthrough in medical research and the energy of your prayers, I'm happy to say, the doctors are predicting my mother will make a complete recovery. Because of the local love and support I first received; the championship bout between the Hammer and myself, will now be held at the Madison Square Garden Arena in NYC. So it will be more economical for those wanting to attend. I love you all."

"Prince? Prince? Do you have a strategy or a defense against the Hammer?"

"To not get hit. We'll think of the rest within four months."

15 minutes later, the Hammer's Q&A session was aired. "... Yes Philly is close, but I'm the New Yorker. Of course, I wanted the fight here. Prince is an extension of Nubs. Nubs is the brilliant strategist. Target Nubs' weaknesses and make Prince have to think for himself. Regardless of what the public's opinion of boxing; boxing is a thinking sport. It's only two percent physical and the other 98

percent is mental. ... Blood is thicker than love."

CHAPTER 56

PRINCE

A painful joy. I wasn't able to study at the hospital anymore, my mother wasn't having it. She'd become active, reaching at objects, crying for attention, playing with her toes, amazed by her fingers. Her innocence was back. It showed in everything she did; her laughter as Phoenix gave her goose berries: blowing bubbles on her cheek like our mother had done us millions of times.

CHAPTER 57

PRINCE

It wasn't my private fight; because I was committed to my family, my family never doubted me and showed their loyalty and dedication and had also accepted the challenge. When my training intensified, everyone in my family pitched in; especially Phoenix, studying film alongside me, pointing out tell-tell signs before the Hammer would throw a punch.

"See it! See it!" The left hook was the Hammer's most powerful punch, and Phoenix had figured out his lunch sequence. "See how he does his feet before releasing his left hook! See it! See it!"

"I see it! I see it!"

Nubs and I spent hours developing a pre-emptive counter to capitalize off of our knowledge.

The people watching my training session thought Phoenix's barking at me and my brothers, was cute, but her foot work drills were more harsh than the sparring: rapidly screaming, "Freak it! Freak it! Wiggle that dance! ..." She changed her rhythm every time I thought I had caught on, so I just listened and went with her flow.

There was only one problem that arose with my training, and it was huge; none of my sparring partners could simulate the Hammer's strength or speed or power. But we worked with what we had.

Precious had turned the store area of our home into an Olympic weight room, which I used constantly since Campbell was too busy studying, preparing for the SAT, and wouldn't sneak over.

CHAPTER 58

PRINCE

A promise, enmeshed to protect and love. The fourth surgery was completed on my mother, everything was going great except one night when the sitter had fallen asleep, my mother scratched at the bandages on her head, which came off and she continued into the wound. The damage was minor, but the doctors requested we restrain her when she was alone and at night.

It was hard to take the screaming and tears, along with my mother reaching out to us for help while the doctors examined her. I saw a concerned look on Dr. Jacob's face as another doctor pointed.

"Is there a problem?"

"There's a little inflammation, caused by her scratching. But there's no sign of infection. I'm going to start her on some antibiotics, which should reduce the inflammation and kill any infection."

The doctors wrapped my mother's head again. When they released the restraints from my mother's hands, my mother hugged Precious and cried herself to sleep.

Each day from then on, my mother became more and more irritated, like a child teething, and would used all of her strength to try to scratch her head. It would take two or three nurses to restrain her, unless Precious was there to stop her and comfort her.

Campbell and I both took the SAT on the same day at the same place. We both felt good about how we had done on the test, so we celebrated by getting a room.

My cell awakened us. It was Precious, "Mama has a fever and these people seem like they don't care. You need to come down here now!"

"Calm down. I'm on my way."

I had called Dr. Jacob, and she met us at the hospital. My mother's temperature was only 99 degrees.

"That's too high!"

"Precious?"

"No Prince, something is wrong with mama! I know. I can tell! Check her bandages. Check her please!"

Dr. Jacob did as told. "It's minor inflammation. Nothing to be concerned over. I'm going to raise the dosage of antibiotics and add a mild sedative."

Precious was cradling our mother as much as she could, rocking with her and softly stroking her face, "We're going to make it better. We're going to make it better."

.....

Time and life seemed to had shifted gears and sped up. There was a month and a half before school was out, and two months until my birthday and the fight. Campbell had talked her mother and stepfather into talking to her father about allowing us to attend the prom together. He agreed under one circumstance; one of his body guards was the limo driver. We lost our chaperon inside the dance. While he was looking for us, we'd snuck back to the limo, and consummated the prom. So, when he refused to take us to a hotel, it didn't matter. Overall, it was a great night.

CHAPTER 59

PRINCE

The value of respect; the simple act can allow people into your life, make your life better and you a better person.

John Henry walked into the gym and no one knew what to expect. Everything stopped. He was fully recovered and looked bigger.

"I heard you're looking for a sparring partner."

Nubs immediately didn't like the idea, but I wasn't about to turn down any help. He was the solution, the answer.

"He's the closest thing we've got to the Hammer's speed and power."

"You'll be too busted up to give a hundred percent against the Hammer! What if you have to meet him again down the road? He'll know too much about you."

"I'll know the same about him."

"I can give you all I know and got, to help you beat the Hammer."

"Why would you do this?"

"I hate Frank Bosco, and I want a contract stating I'll be the first person you defend your title against."

"I can't. It's a guaranteed rematch in my contract."

"He gave you that?"

"He had no choice. We can draw up a contract that you'll be the second or I'll give you five million dollars for 30 days of your services."

Nubs bugged his eyes at me, "You don't even pay me that much!

"I pay you more than that!"

"I thought we were working together!"

I ignored Nubs. John Henry's knowledge was more valuable than trying to be cheap, "John Henry, it's in your corner."

"I want the second title bout."

Nubs had to kick people out and close the gym when John Henry and I sparred. The crowd would fill the street, watching through the glass front.

Half of the session was walk throughs, counters and defenses. The last half was full speed; showing what I'd learned or getting it beat into me. Hard work isn't pretty or glamorous or even fun, but it prepares you to win.

We both took our lumps and the crowd size grew until Nubs ordered limo tint installed on the glass front.

John Henry was a decent man who kept the bar set high and loved his wife. She would fly in for the weekends and jet out Monday mornings. John would shine every time he spoke of her. He was an impressive guy and we became good friends. He would come to the house and workout with me.

We both were striving for excellence, the persistent pursuit to become better, giving our all at everything, at all times trying to improve. We were competitive, but at that moment it wasn't about winning or losing; it was that we identified with certain situations and understood undoubtable feelings.

"Big J, why do you hate Bosco so? What did he do?"

"It's what I did. I sold him my soul. I was an up and coming fighter, and he flashed the big deal and promises. But once I joined his stable he hid me. He kept me out front, but guided me away from the championship bouts, using me to clear a path for the Hammer."

"But he made you rich and gave you a shot at the Hammer."

"I underestimated both of them; The power and the influence Bosco has, and the skill level of the Hammer. Kid, you're the greatest fighter I've ever fought, and you're right; don't leave it in anyone else's hands, when you can do it yourself. Don't underestimate them."

"If you think I'm the greatest, what makes you think you'll ever beat me?"

"Because I'm greater!

CHAPTER 60

PRINCE

The mild sedative kept my mother mellow, but her motions were of someone in agony.

Even though school wasn't officially out, Precious had completed all of her examines, so she spent almost 23 hours a day at the hospital, beside our mother.

It was three days before graduation, the date of my mother's fifth surgery. The doctors were in the room prepping my mother for surgery. My mother was almost under but was still reaching for us.

Precious went to her, kissing her face and crying with her. "It's going to be all right. They're going to stop the pain. We'll be right here when you return. Go to sleep. I love you mama."

We all gave our mother hugs and kisses and told her, I love you, before she went under and the orderlies pushed the bed out of the room.

Precious and Phoenix cried in my arms. "She's going to be fine."

We sat in my mother's hospital room for 14 hours, only moving to go to the bathroom. The door opened and all the air seemed to have instantly left the room. It was Dr. Jacob, and no sign of the orderlies returning with our mother.

Precious' voice trembled out, "Where's our mother? Where's my mama?"

The solemn look of the doctor made Precious break down. I grabbed Precious and she cried into my chest. I couldn't understand how it had happened. "What happened? She'd made so much improvement?"

Dr. Jacob, she looked at me, my tears, my brothers and my sisters' tears. "An infection had spread throughout her brain, and had caused major swelling. Her brain just shut down during the surgery."

Precious tried to pull away from me, to get at the doctor, "You stupid cow! I told you months ago something was wrong with her! If you would've listened, my mother would be alive right now! You killed her! You killed her!"

Tears fell from Dr. Jacob's eyes as she shook her head, then backed out of the room.

Things had changed that rapidly. There wasn't time to grieve. I had over 100 million dollars, but I was only 17. My family was at risk of being separated since we didn't have a legal guardian.

"We have to go, Let's go."

"What about mama?"

"We don't have to be here to make the burial arrangements. Come on!"

As we left, I saw the doctor we'd replaced, on his cell, watching the corridor and my mother's room. The way he was eyeing us, made me think whatever he was discussing was pertaining to us.

I didn't want to drop Phoenix, Pharaoh and Phihiem off at the gym, but I had a gut feeling about that doctor.

Precious and I continued to our house. An unmarked Charger and the social worker were waiting outside our home. I recognized Agent Sader inside the unmarked car.

"Where're the children?"

Precious and I ignored the social worker, and closed the door in her face.

The connections we'd made at the foundations' openings paid off. I called the mayor who immediately returned my call. He was genuinely sympathetic over my family's lost, then made a call to a judge.

The unmarked car followed us to the judge's home at eleven o'clock at night. Nubs' van was out front.

The judge was a boxing fan, once being a golden glove himself. Phoenix and my brothers were playing with two huge puppies, massive hounds, while the judge and Nubs had a drink, talking shop. After a few pictures, the judge signed a predated guardianship order, making me the legal guardian of Phoenix, Pharaoh and Phihiem, with a clause; if something was to happen to me, Nubs would automatically become their legal guardian until Precious became of age. The judge then gave his condolences and wished me good luck in the fight.

·····

The weight of life sunk in on me when I stretched out across my mother's bed. I felt crushed, pinned, boxed in. I didn't want to breathe. For three days I stayed in bed, grieving my mother. I missed my graduation, and didn't care about the fight. All I remember is the curtains being pulled open, blinding me with sunlight, then Campbell's image came into focus.

"Get up. Get up! You can't give up now! Not after all you've been through. Not after all you've said. There're people counting on you!"

"She's gone. She's gone. My mother is dead!"

"Yes, but you're here! You have to stay strong! People are counting on you. You can't give up!" Her voice cracked from becoming emotional. "... Look! Look out of this window."

I wasn't going to move, I didn't want to. My brothers and sisters were watching from the door way to the room. Phoenix entered and walked to the window, then silently held out her hand to me. My little sister led me to the window. Thousands of flowers cluttered the side walk and street, along with signs wishing us the best. Candles had burnt down to only wax, People, strangers, different skin colors, genders, relaying the same message; dropping off more flowers, cards and candles, feeling connected to me, my family. They saw me and my family as an extension of them; I realized they were my extended family. My difficult times had become theirs, the same as my success was theirs. It wasn't about individuality, but a shared experience of all of us together.

.....

Precious had arranged the funeral procession. It was held at the study hall instead of a church, more in accordance to my mother's belief. It only held 1100 people, so many people paid their respect in the street outside the hall, listening to Cuda Bay's lecture, broadcasted over the loud speakers, "When you die, people like to lie for you, to build you up. But while you're alive, people tend to lie on you. But the life we live speaks for us. The customary thing to do after a death is an autopsy for the cause of death, but the smart thing to do would be an autopsy of life; learn from death how to live. Sister Battle's life is a prime example to us. Her energy, an indestructible source, endlessly changing to overcome circumstances, divinely guided to raise five beautiful children.

Cultivation, culmination. A conduction. A continuance. A natural resource producing power, with the capacity to stimulate, reproduce growth, be it physically, mentally, spiritually, socially or financially. Sister Battle's time period from birth continues to exist in every form of our true understanding. When a star dies, its light doesn't fade. It spreads through time, Greatness lives on. ..."

Below the podium was a huge portrait of my mother at her best with the urn containing her ashes next to it.

Mr. Bosco, Campbell and his two body guards were in attendance. Campbell released her father's hand and he allowed her to come to me.

Cuda Bay closed and nurse Pottier sang 'Precious Lord' as the community and the city showed their respect and support, rotating past the portrait, giving their condolences.

Cuda Bay and his family were the last, "You are a strong man. Greatness awaits you." As he ended his statement he gave me a compassionate hug.

CHAPTER 61

CUDA BAY

Looking for flaws. I'd given up on finding the crack in the damn. I had a lecture prepared but when I went to address the audience at the study hall, I saw Prince and his family sitting there. The subject matter seemed irrelevant. "... It's hard to admit greatness. Envy blinds you, especially when you're doing everything in and beyond your power to achieve greatness. Even when we look back at all the ones that have made the strides and seemed to have been great. We compare then to now, pros to cons, and we still want to deny his or her greatness. But you keep recognizing it, in its smallest detail to its largest element. Because we critique everything, searching for flaws; because it's so hard to believe it's possible, and if so, why I couldn't achieve it? I know this from personal experience. I had to come to terms with there's someone greater than me. I'm not going to persecute, I'm going to do what's right. I'm going to encourage greatness, support greatness and try my best to strive along with greatness. ..."

The community, every aspect, every sacrifice, had summed up to create Prince, and he personified it. The community was proud to have him stand on our shoulders.

"... Greatness motivates without trying, creates without knowing. A present even when you're not in its presence. I'm not a preacher, I'm a lecturer, but I feel happy, happy that I have been honored to witness this young man's courage, strength, wisdom and every positive attribute mentionable! ..." I'd tried to kill him, and in return he'd spared my life; given me my freedom and sent the revenue earnings of my company beyond the atmosphere. And he still appeared to be that humble big kid.

CHAPTER 62

PRINCE

Blinded by the hype. I was in the best physical shape ever. I had the world's sympathy, and Vegas and the media had me favored, painting the picture for the public that I was on a mission to win it for my mother. The notion had crept into my head, and the last seven days before the fight I trained for that mission. I allowed the Hammer to do all the jaw-jacking at the press conference. My bulk and definition thrilled the press at the weigh-in.

.....

At ring side, a reporter stopped Campbell instead of Mr. Bosco, "Who are you pulling for?"

"Me?"

"You're Campbell Bosco, sister of the Hammer and Prince's girl-friend?"

"Yes."

"Who are you pulling for?"

"I love them both. I wish there was a way for both of them to win."

"You didn't answer the question?"

"I'm going to be happy for whoever wins, and sad for whoever loses. But they're both champions to me."

The body guards then blocked the path of the reporter and the camera crew as Mr. Bosco and Campbell took their seats.

.....

Mrs. Bay had delivered a new satin robe and boxers, along with matching trainers' jackets for Nubs, Pharaoh, Phihiem and even one designed to fit Phoenix – all, one third red, white and blue, with a gold lion stepping through a gold crown on the center of the back. My boxers were identical, except the gold lion and crown were in the center of the front of the waist band.

A kiss on Phoenix's forehead, two rock hard pounds to my brothers, then I left them watching the pre-fight on the television in the locker room.

I knew the Hammer's tell signs. I knew his counter moves. I knew his strengths and his very few weaknesses. Mentally and physically I felt ready, but when the bell rang the ring didn't teleport in my mind. The flashes, the noise. I wasn't focused, still I pressed on, but it was like the Hammer was clairvoyant, beating me to the punch, bobbing, ducking, getting out before I could sprang my traps.

Round after round he was out thinking us, out boxing me, eating away at my faith in me, my confidence, my will.

Between rounds Nubs stayed at me, trying to keep me motivated, "Dig, dig! You'll get him!"

Everything we tried seemed not to be working, then when we thought something was working and we'd fought back in it; punching, taking blows, giving blows: I got knocked back on my ass. I didn't see the punch coming, so it hurt like crazy. The fall itself almost knocked me out. I hit the mat so hard.

.....

In the locker room Phoenix kicked the stool and toppled the television, then ran out, followed by my brothers. She was running and screaming toward the ring, "Get up! Get up."

Security recognized the trainers' jackets and allowed them to my corner. My brothers were pounding on the mat, yelling, spitting with every word, "Get up! Get up!"

Everything was fuzzy and distorted; their facial expressions, their eyes, their body language.

The ref was at six in his count.

Precious and Mrs. Bay had tears running down their faces as they screamed for me to, "Get up!"

Beckon's had chartered busses and brought almost the entire community, which was begging, screaming, praying for me to, "Get the fuck up!"

It fueled me. I was on my feet by nine. I was damaged, but I showed the ref I had control of my motor skills, and he continued the fight.

The Hammer moved in for the kill with body blows that lifted me off the mat, even though I was tucked tight.

I distinctively heard Phoenix's voice crying, "Fight back! Fight back!"

Nubs' words were jumbled in with the roar of the crowd, "12 more seconds!"

But as clear as a bell, Phoenix's voice kept ringing, "Fight back! Fight back!"

Punches were coming from every direction. The Hammer was trying to finish me. I couldn't risk exposing myself. I survived the round.

Pharaoh and Phihiem jumped into the ring and help me to the corner. Nubs was checking me for a concussion, "What day is your birthday?"

"Today!"

"How do you feel?"

"Like he's kicking my ass."

"Yeah, that's about right."

It hurt me to laugh. Phoenix didn't find anything funny. She was the embodiment of enthusiasm. "Have you given up! You're not fighting back! You and mom said we don't give up! So, fight back!"

She, tomorrow and now, was my spiritual connection to the past, and my reason to continue to fight for the future. She was my undying will; despite the difficulties I was having she wouldn't allow my spirit to be defeated. She was right: I wasn't fighting to win. I was fighting not to lose, and as a result I was being out boxed.

"... Are you listening to me? Listen to me!" The bell rang.

"I'm listening."

"Then listen! ... Dance! Dance! I said dance Prince!"

I realized she wanted me to do the footwork drills.

"... Dance! Dance! ..." Both right hooks landed, stunning the Hammer. "... Dance!

Dance! ..." The body blows landed, but the Hammer blocked the head shot. "... Freak it! Freak it! ..." The left to the body broke something, and the left to his head sent him backwards. "... Wiggle with it! Wiggle with it! ... Freak it! Freak that wiggle! Freak that wiggle!" I bobbed and weaved, then slid back to the right, releasing a double up of right hooks. I immediately, bobbed and weaved and slid to the left, lunching a left to the body, then the head. The combo floored him.

The crowd cheered, but I knew he wouldn't stay down. He was more mad than hurt. He jabbed off the cobwebs.

"... Dance! Dance! Freak it! Freak it!" The hooks drove him to the ropes.

He jabbed me, then hugged me tightly, making the ref give a warning before he let go; eating up as much time as he could, then got on his bicycle to end the round.

The momentum had swung in my direction. The Hammer's corner was on his ass. The problem was; it wasn't Nubs or myself doing the thinking, it was Phoenix that had them dumbfounded. Nubs kissed Phoenix's forehead, "You're a goddamn genius!"

"You're just realizing that!"

"When you slid, be conscious of his short uppercut."

The bell rang and the ring teleported us to the warriors' dimension. I was focused; only the Hammer and I surrounded by darkness with the divine voice of Phoenix singing instructions. She was my maestro, keeping my level of intensity up. My power blows were doing major damage. The Hammer's defense was the jab, but his determination wouldn't allow him to fall. The bell brought back the chaos of Nubs' screaming at me in my corner, "Why you didn't finish him!"

"I'm trying! I'm hitting him with all I've got!"

Phoenix was eyeing the Hammer's corner; his trainer, screaming at him, him screaming at his trainer.

"Look, look! You got them arguing." Phoenix was right.

I pounded on the Hammer for the next three rounds. He simply refused to go down. His resilience, his dogged determination to fight to win.

"Kept chopping, he'll fall!" Nubs pushed me out of the corner as the bell transported us.

Hooks and jabs, Hooks and jabs. My hooks guided him, his jabs stopped me from finishing him.

It was a remix in the middle of Phoenix's song. I was sliding to the left, coming out of my bob when I heard, "Blue!" being screamed. I saw the right upper cut coming. All I could do was fade back. It wasn't flush, but it caught me on the corner of my chin with enough power to lock the nerves in my body. I wasn't out, but it seemed like I was falling from heaven until the ropes caught me.

The darkness surrounding us became scenes from my life; my mother kissing me bye before leaving with Shey and Precious; Stopping my brothers from robbing the white boy; Phoenix crying, screaming at her classmates to tell the truth; finding

Precious badly beaten and raped; my mother in her hospital bed, reaching out for me; Campbell drawing back the curtains revealing the light; Phoenix holding out her hand to me; ways of expressed love, that needed push.

I took a standing eight. The cobwebs were thick, but I knew the Hammer was a head hunter, so instead of retreating, I bobbed right and threw a blind hard right to his gut, that made him buckle. I was too dazed to get on my bicycle, so I stood my ground. He was just as hurt from the hook. We both stood still the last six seconds of the eleventh round.

I shook off the stool and stood, watching as the Hammer did the same. It wasn't a mind game on my part; I didn't have the energy to waste sitting, then getting back up.

"The rounds could be even, but he has two knock downs."

"I'm going to decide this, one way or the other."

The fans were standing for the last round. The bell transported us. I was bobbing and weaving to the center of the ring.

"Dance! Dance!" Instead of a right, I threw two lefts that landed; because the Hammer tucked to his left – like I'd figured, he and his corner had figured out what Phoenix's instructions meant. The blows rocked him, but he snapped back with a deep upper cut that I barely stepped out of its reach.

He'd stopped me from closing for the kill. Jabs and hooks, and upper cuts. We both knew how to defend against them. Both bicycles were thrown away. No one was retreating. I'd been boxing since I was eight; the Hammer, since he was eleven. We had over 25 years of combined experience, and we were using the knowledge of every second of it. What I knew and what I knew he knew. Toe-to-toe, blocking and countering, punching and ducking, looking for an opening, an edge.

Both corners screamed. "20 seconds left!"

The Hammer threw safety out of the ring and risked it all. He hadn't thrown his notorious left hook the entire fight. My eyes automatically sent the alarm to my brain, which fired an overhand right at the thought of the Hammer setting his feet before releasing his left hook, his most powerful weapon. He was about to pull the trigger when my bomb landed flush on his temple. He went down, but caught the bottom rope as both of his knees hit the mat. I could tell he wasn't out, because he was reaching for the middle rope. It could've been instincts, until he grabbed it, then the top rope, pulling himself up. I knew what he was feeling; it was as if we had to win or die than lose.

The ref was still counting, "Six, seven, ..." The Hammer was trying to shake the cobwebs loose as he managed to sturdy his hands for the ref who stopped his count on, "Nine!" and continued the fight as the bell rang ending the fight.

The crowd couldn't believe it, because it was unbelievable; the entire left side of the Hammer's face had instantly ballooned and his eye was swollen shut, but I agreed with the ref's call to continue the fight. We both had given our all and refused to submit to defeat. Neither one of us deserved to lose.

The arena was silent as the judges read their score of the fight. The first judge had the fight even. The second judge also had the fight as a draw. The final judge made me the winner by one point. I threw a kiss to my mother, then I also raised the Hammer's arm. I cried as I embraced Phoenix and my brothers, then Nubs.

Precious was standing crying and clapping. I was trying to scream over the noise for her to come to the ring. "Precious! Precious!"

Nubs was crying while polishing and kissing the championship belt.

Precious pulled Campbell to the ring with her. Campbell kissed her brother first, then ran to my arms. "You did it!"

Precious, Phoenix and my brothers all hugged us, "We did it!"

A new beginning, never the end.